True Tales™
from the
Jungles

Henry Billings

Melissa Stone Billings

STECK-VAUGHN
ELEMENTARY · SECONDARY · ADULT · LIBRARY

A Harcourt Company

www.steck-vaughn.com

Acknowledgments

Executive Editor: Stephanie Muller
Senior Editor: Kristy Schulz
Project Editor: Meredith Edgley O'Reilly
Associate Director of Design: Cynthia Ellis
Design Manager: Alexandra Corona
Media Researcher: Claudette Landry
Electronic Production Artists: Dina Instinski, Linda Reed
Electronic Production Specialist: Alan Klemp

Cartography: MapQuest.com, Inc.
Illustration Credits: Pp. 8, 65 Kathie Kelleher
Photo Credits: Cover (inset) ©Stephan Schwartzman/National Wildlife Federation; Cover (background), p.1 CORBIS/Wolfgang Kaehler; Cover (hat, compass, passport), p.3 ©PhotoDisc; p.6 CORBIS/Wolfgang Kaehler; p.9(l) CORBIS/Michael & Patricia Fogden; p.9(r) CORBIS/Gary Braasch; p.10 ©North Wind Picture Archives; pp.14, 16 The Granger Collection; p.17 Taylor & Dull/The Menil Collection, Houston; p.18 ©PhotoDisc; p.22 ©E.R. Degginger/DEGG1/Bruce Coleman, Inc.; p.24 Brown Brothers; p.25(t) Fiala, Anthony/NGS Image Collection; p.25(b) Archive Photos; p.26 Culver Pictures; p.30 CORBIS/Bettmann; p.32 Culver Pictures; p.33 Archive Photos; p.34 CORBIS/Hulton-Deutsch Collection; pp.38, 40–42 ©Jesse Page; p.46 ©David Austen/Tony Stone Images; pp.48–49 CORBIS/Bettmann-UPI; p.50 CORBIS/Hulton-Deutsch Collection; p.54 CORBIS/Staffan Widstrand; p.56 CORBIS/Yann Arthus-Bertrand; p.57 ©Watkins/Sipa Press; p.58 (both) CORBIS/Yann Arthus-Bertrand; p.62 CORBIS/Michael S. Yamashita; p.64 CORBIS/Bettmann; p.66 Hulton Getty/Liaison Agency, Inc.; p.70 CORBIS/Yann Arthus-Bertrand; p.72 ©Carl Frank/Photo Researchers; p.73 ©Tony Stone Images; p.74 ©Gamma Liaison; p.78 ©Mark Newman/Adventure Photo & Film; p.80 Mattis Klum/NGS/Image Collection; p.81–2 Reuters/Goh Chai Hin/Archive Photos; p.86 ©Photri-Microstock; pp.88–89 ©PHOTRI; p.90 Courtesy Mrs. Alberta Tillman; p.94 ©Photo Researchers; p.96 CORBIS/Gian Berto Vanni; p.97 CORBIS/Charles & Josette Lenars; p.98 ©Robert Lubeck/Animals Animals; p.108(t) ©Jacques Langoux/Tony Stone Images; p.108(m) CORBIS/Michael & Patricia Fogden; p.108(b) CORBIS/Wolfgang Kaehler; p.109(t) ©Nigel J.H.Smith/Earth Scenes; p.109(m) CORBIS/Darren Maybury, Eye Ubiquitous; p.109(b) CORBIS/Johnathan Smith, Cordaiy Photo Library.

ISBN 0-7398-0853-2

Contents

Tropical Jungle

NORTH
AMERICA

ATLANTIC
OCEAN

Mississippi River

Yellow
River

Crane Branch
Swamp

PACIFIC
OCEAN

El Cayo
Ruins

Rio Bobonaza

Equator

Xapuri

SOUTH
AMERICA

ATLANTIC
OCEAN

MAP KEY
▨ Tropical Jungle

f the World

ARCTIC
OCEAN

EUROPE

ASIA

PACIFIC

OCEAN

FRICA

GUAM

Virunga
Mts.

Mt. Kinabalu

Congo River

BORNEO

NEW
GUINEA

mbaréné

Tana
River

INDIAN

OCEAN

AUSTRALIA

N

W   E

S

ANTARCTICA

Lost in the Rain Forest

Isabela Godin had not seen her husband in twenty years. Now, at last, she had the chance to join him. To do so, Isabela would have to travel down South America's Rio Bobonaza. This river cuts through Ecuador and Peru. It leads through miles of thick jungle. Isabela didn't think the trip would be easy. But she had no idea just how terrible it would be.

Getting Started

For years, Isabela and her husband Jean had lived in what today is Ecuador. But in 1749, they decided to move to France, where Jean had been born. To get there, they would travel across South America to French Guiana. Then they would travel across the Atlantic Ocean to France.

Jean left first, hoping Isabela would soon join him. He waited in French Guiana for her. But Jean had had trouble getting **permission** to travel across South America. Twenty years passed before Isabela also was allowed to make the journey.

At last, Isabela got permission to go. She took forty people with her. This included two of her brothers, her 12-year-old **nephew,** and many servants. In 1769 the group began their journey, heading for French Guiana. There Jean was waiting.

The group started off on foot. For sixty miles, they walked through the mountains. At last, they came to the Rio Bobonaza, a **tributary** of the Amazon River.

The group planned to follow the Rio Bobonaza to the Amazon River. Then they would follow the Amazon River across the **continent**.

Isabela went to the river town of Canelos. She planned to hire Indian guides to lead her down the Rio Bobonaza. Then she would just sit back in a canoe and relax. But it didn't work out the way she hoped.

Down the River

When Isabela got to Canelos, the place was empty. The disease **smallpox** had swept through the village. Many people had died. The rest had run away in fear. Isabela's servants got scared. Most of them ran off, too. Only Isabela and ten others kept going.

For a while, they did all right. They found an Indian to help them. Although he was quite sick, he agreed to act as their guide down the river. But then he fell into the water. He didn't have the strength to swim back to the canoe. Isabela's group watched helplessly as he drowned in the deep water.

Now the group was really in trouble. They were days away from the nearest village. No one knew how

Isabela Godin didn't know how hard her journey would be.

At night, vampire bats attacked Isabela's group.

to steer the canoe. Soon, the canoe tipped over. The group struggled to get on land. Then Isabela sent three men down the river to get help. She and the others stayed behind at the edge of the river.

For four weeks, Isabela waited for help to come. But slowly, the group ran out of food. They dug up roots to eat. They killed and ate a couple of birds. But each day, they grew weaker. Some were sick from disease. At night, **vampire bats** attacked them. The bats sucked blood from the people's bare feet as they slept.

At last, Isabela realized help might never come. The eight people would have to save themselves. They built a **raft** and tried to float down the river. But they hit a log. The raft fell apart. Once again, the group stood at the edge of the river, soaking wet.

Through the Jungle

In **desperation,** Isabela told everyone to start walking. But the jungle was full of vines and trees. Everywhere they turned, they saw strange plants and tangled bushes. The air was hot and steamy. Bugs crawled on them. Soon their bare feet were bleeding. Branches tore their clothing and scratched their faces. There was no fresh water to drink. They became lost in this thick **rain forest**.

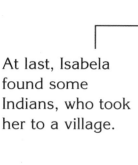
At last, Isabela found some Indians, who took her to a village.

At last, even Isabela was ready to quit. The small group sank down to the jungle floor, too tired to take another step. They were sick and starving. Within hours, Isabela's nephew was dead. One by one, the others also died. Soon only Isabela was alive. For two days, she lay there next to the bodies of her family and servants.

Then, somehow, she found the strength to get up. She began to drag herself through the jungle once more. Her husband later described what happened. "On her second day of walking... she found some water and, during the next few days, some wild fruit and green eggs...." She had been hungry for so long that she could barely swallow. Still, she was able to eat enough to stay alive.

After nine days of wandering through the **dense** vines and trees, Isabela came across some Indians near the river. They were shocked to see this half-dead woman crawl out of the jungle. They helped her into their canoe and took her to a village.

Although Isabela was very weak, she chose to continue her journey. At last, she reached French Guiana. There she was able to join her husband and share with him her amazing story. Then, in 1773 they finally moved to France, where they stayed for the rest of their lives.

USE WHAT YOU KNOW

Read and Remember — Finish the Sentence

Circle the best ending for each sentence.

1. Isabela Godin planned to travel down the Rio Bobonaza by _____.
   walking along it   riding in a canoe   riding in a French ship

2. At Canelos, most of Godin's servants _____.
   ran away   drowned   got smallpox

3. No one in Godin's group knew how to _____.
   cook   steer a canoe   speak French

4. Isabela was rescued by _____.
   her nephew   Indians   French soldiers

5. Isabela and her husband finally moved to _____.
   France   Ecuador   French Guiana

Think About It — Drawing Conclusions

Write one or more sentences to answer each question.

1. Why did Isabela Godin want to get to French Guiana? _____

   _____

2. Why did Godin's servants become scared when they reached

   Canelos? _____

3. What are two reasons Godin's group became weaker each day?_____

   _____

   _____

4. Why did Isabela's group try to float down the river on a raft? _____

   _____

Focus on Vocabulary — Finish the Paragraphs

Use the words in dark print to complete the paragraphs. Reread the paragraphs to be sure they make sense.

smallpox	**vampire bats**	**permission**	**nephew**
raft	**tributary**	**desperation**	**rain forest**
dense	**continent**		

Isabela Godin wanted to travel across the (1)_____ of South America to French Guiana. In 1769 she finally got (2)_____ to go. She took servants and family members with her, including her 12-year-old (3)_____. The group planned to travel down the Rio Bobonaza. This river is a (4)_____ of the Amazon River. First, they went to the town of Canelos to find guides. But the disease (5)_____ had swept through it. Still, Godin and ten others continued on the journey.

Godin sent three men down the river to get help. The rest of the group became weak and sick as they waited. At night, (6)_____ bit their toes. After waiting four weeks, Godin's group built a (7)_____ and tried to float down the river. But they hit a log and ended up in the river. At last, in (8)_____ they tried to walk through the steamy (9)_____. They got lost in the (10)_____ tangle of vines, trees, and plants. One by one the people in the group died. In the end, only Isabela made it to French Guiana.

Continents and Oceans

Isabela Godin traveled across the **continent** of South America. A continent is a large body of land. Earth also has large bodies of water called oceans. Look at the map of the world below. Write the answer to each question.

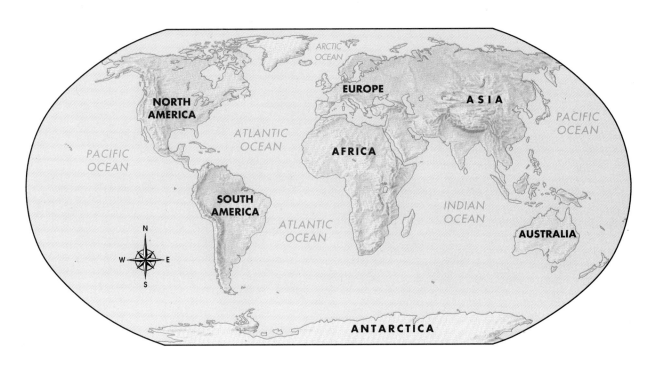

1. What are the names of the seven continents? _____

   _____

2. Which three continents are along both the Atlantic Ocean and the

   Pacific Ocean? _____

3. Which two oceans are along Europe? _____

4. Which two oceans are along Australia? _____

5. Along which four continents is the Indian Ocean? _____

   _____

6. Which ocean is found between Africa and South America? _____

   _____

African Adventurer

Mary Kingsley was tired of her quiet life in England. She wanted to see new sights and meet new people. So in 1893 she headed for the **region** of West Africa. Her friends thought she was crazy. In those days, people from Europe didn't know much about Africa. To them, it was a strange and deadly place. In fact, ships didn't even sell round-trip tickets to Africa. People who went to explore the continent's jungles were expected never to return.

Bugs, Snakes, and Crocodiles

Kingsley was not frightened by what she saw in the **coastal** region of West Africa. In fact, she enjoyed herself. She met many interesting people. She lived through wild storms. She even learned to eat bugs, snakes, and crocodiles.

The next year, Kingsley decided to make a longer **expedition** through West Africa. She hired a few African men to go with her. Then she headed up the Ogooué River through what today is the country of Gabon. She would be traveling in areas that no European had traveled in before.

At first, Kingsley's group had to paddle their long canoes through **swamps**. These low, wet places were dotted with trees and hanging vines. The swamps were quiet during the day. But at night, they seemed to come alive.

"After dark it is full of noises," Kingsley wrote. There were grunts from **unknown** creatures. There were splashes from jumping fish. There were creaking

Kingsley and her group traveled on the Ogooué River in long canoes.

sounds from trees. Above all, there was the strange sigh of crocodiles.

Early one morning, a crocodile attacked Kingsley. It threw its front legs into her canoe. Kingsley knew the creature would eat her if it got the chance. She grabbed her paddle and hit the crocodile on its head. Luckily for her, it slipped back into the water and swam away. Bravely, Kingsley continued on the expedition.

Deeper into the Jungle

Soon, Kingsley saw the land change. The river cut through deep forests. When the group stopped to rest, Kingsley often took a walk around. But she was careful not to go near Fang villages. Europeans did not know much about the Fang. But Kingsley had heard that they were an angry and dangerous people.

During one walk, Kingsley stepped on a patch of green leaves. It gave way, and she found herself falling through a deep hole. Kingsley had stepped on the roof of a home built into a **hollow**. The home belonged to a Fang family. She later wrote, "I am pretty sure they were not expecting me to drop in." Still, she made friends with them. She found that they were not the terrible people she had expected them to be. She searched her pockets and gave the family a few gifts, such as handkerchiefs. Then she continued on her way.

Kingsley and her group traveled farther down the river. Later, they left their canoes. They walked deeper into the jungle. Now Kingsley worried about new dangers. Gorillas roamed freely. So did leopards. Scorpions crawled along the ground. Huge snakes hung from trees.

Dangers Everywhere

One day, Kingsley got caught in a **tornado** and a rainstorm. "The **fierce** rain came in a roar," she wrote. During this storm, Kingsley almost drowned while crossing a stream. She climbed under some rocks to get out of the rain. But she was not alone. Just three feet away was a big leopard. "He was **crouching** on the ground with his head thrown back and his eyes shut," she wrote.

These two masks were made by members of a Fang tribe.

Luckily, the leopard did not notice Kingsley. It was too busy worrying about the storm. For twenty minutes the two of them stayed there. At last, the storm passed, and the leopard ran off.

Through all her travels, Kingsley wore a long wool skirt, fancy boots, and a black hat. This might have seemed like strange clothing for the jungle. But it came in handy. One day, Kingsley stepped on a pile of bushes that hid an elephant trap. She fell through the bushes into a large hole that was 15 feet deep. At the bottom of the hole were many sharp **spikes**. Each one was a foot long. "It is at times like these you realize the blessings of a good thick skirt," Kingsley wrote. If she had been wearing thin cotton pants, she would have been "spiked to the bone." As it was, she was not really hurt at all.

At last, Kingsley finished her journey. She returned to England. There she gave many speeches, telling of her travels. She wrote three books about them. Her work helped people in Europe see that Africa was not a strange and deadly place. Instead, it was filled with beauty and life.

Kingsley saw leopards, scorpions, and crocodiles during her journey.

Read and Remember — Check the Events

Place a check in front of the three sentences that tell what happened in the story.

_____ **1.** Mary Kingsley fell through the roof of a Fang family's house.

_____ **2.** Kingsley tried to keep Europeans out of Africa.

_____ **3.** Kingsley wanted to find a crocodile, but she never saw one.

_____ **4.** Kingsley's thick skirt kept her safe from sharp spikes in an elephant trap.

_____ **5.** During a tornado, a leopard in a cave attacked Kingsley.

_____ **6.** Kingsley traveled up Gabon's Ogooué River.

Write About It

Imagine you were Mary Kingsley. Write a letter to a friend in England, describing how you feel as you travel through the jungles of Gabon.

Dear _____,

_____

_____

_____

_____

_____

_____

_____

Focus on Vocabulary — Match Up

Match each word with its meaning. Write the correct letter on the blank.

_____ **1.** region

_____ **2.** expedition

_____ **3.** crouching

_____ **4.** coastal

_____ **5.** tornado

_____ **6.** spikes

_____ **7.** hollow

_____ **8.** fierce

_____ **9.** swamps

_____ **10.** unknown

a. place where the ground dips

b. whirling storm with strong, high-speed winds

c. lands that are wet, soft, and muddy

d. an area of land

e. long, sharp pieces of wood or metal

f. not familiar

g. near a seashore

h. bending low

i. long journey

j. strong and dangerous

USE A MAP

Map Directions

The four main directions are **north**, **south**, **east**, and **west**. On maps they are shown on a **compass rose**. In-between directions are **northeast**, **southeast**, **southwest**, and **northwest**. The map below shows part of Africa, the continent across which Mary Kingsley traveled. Study the map. Circle the answer that best completes each sentence below.

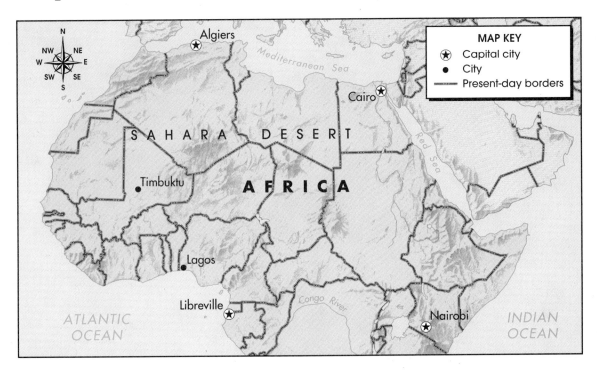

1. Algiers is _____ of the Sahara Desert.

   south   north   west

2. Nairobi is _____ of the Congo River.

   east   west   south

3. Libreville is _____ of Lagos.

   southeast   northwest   southwest

4. Cairo is _____ of Timbuktu.

   northwest   southeast   northeast

River of Doubt

Theodore Roosevelt called the journey his "last chance to be a boy." The **former** President of the United States always had loved adventure. Now, at the age of 55, Teddy Roosevelt was about to begin the adventure of his life. He joined an expedition headed to the country of Brazil in South America. There he would help explore and map a mysterious river called the River of Doubt.

Into the Jungle

The head of the expedition was a Brazilian Indian. His name was Candido Mariano da Silva Rondon. Rondon was a leader in Brazil's army. In 1909 he had seen a strange river flowing north. It wasn't on any map. Yet it was huge. Rondon called it "Rio da Dúvida," or River of Doubt. He thought it might be a tributary of the Madeira River, which flowed into the Amazon River. In 1913 he decided to plan a canoe trip down the river to see where it went.

Rondon took 21 men with him. Among them were co-leader Teddy Roosevelt and his 24-year-old son Kermit. The group reached the river's **headwaters** on February 26, 1914. They knew that as they traveled down the river, they would face **poisonous** insects and snakes, deadly **piranha** fish, and terrible diseases. None of them knew what else lay ahead. Roosevelt said they were going "into the unknown."

Even so, Roosevelt enjoyed his first few days on the river. The water was calm. Roosevelt loved the smell of the plants and the sound of bird songs. He loved the way the jungle "rose like a green wall" on both sides of the river. He also loved how vines looped and twisted from trees "like great ropes."

Soon, however, the beautiful river turned ugly. The **current** grew stronger. The men could hear the roar of **rapids** ahead. The water dropped quickly over steep rocks. At one point it rushed through an opening that was just six feet wide. There was no way to float through that in canoes!

The men now had to **portage,** or carry, their canoes and supplies. They chopped a trail through the dense **vegetation**. Then they cut hundreds of small logs. They used these logs as rollers to move the canoes along the trail. It was very hard work. They were stung by ants and mosquitoes as they worked. It took the men two-and-a-half days to get past these rapids.

From Bad to Worse

This was just a warning of what lay ahead. On March 6, they ran into more rapids. This time it took them three days to portage their equipment. Then

Teddy Roosevelt sits in a canoe, ready to explore the river.

The rapids were swift and dangerous.

Kermit Roosevelt

came a third set of rapids. At that point, the men unloaded the canoes. Some men carried the supplies through the steamy jungle. Others walked the canoes through the rapids. It was dangerous work. But it seemed easier than taking the canoes over land.

On March 15, the group hit swift rapids again. Just then Kermit, who was in the lead canoe, spotted an island. He and two other men went to see if the river was calmer on the other side of the island. It wasn't. They got trapped in a **whirlpool**. Waves pounded the canoe and finally tipped it over.

One of the men made it safely to shore. The second man went under and was never seen again. Kermit managed to save himself by grabbing onto a tree branch that hung over the river.

Farther along, the rapids grew even worse. Again the men had to portage. Rondon and his dog went first. Suddenly, the dog fell dead. An unseen Indian had killed it with an arrow. It gave the men a creepy feeling to know they were being watched from the jungle's bushes. They rushed along as fast as possible.

The End of the Journey

For the next four weeks, the men came upon one set of rapids after another. Everyone grew tired. The food supply ran low. Some of the men came down with high fevers. One day Roosevelt hurt his leg. It had to be cut open in order for the wound to be cleaned out. Then Roosevelt got a high fever. For 48 hours, he was nearly out of his mind.

When the fever broke, Roosevelt called to his son. He told Kermit to go on without him. "I feel I am only a **burden** to the party," he said. But Kermit wouldn't leave his father. He worked harder than ever to get the canoes past the last set of rapids.

On April 27, 1914, the men reached a tiny village. Rondon was right. The river did flow into the Madeira. Roosevelt's last great adventure was over. His body had paid a price, however. He had lost 35 pounds. The fever had turned him into an old man. After returning, he lived just five more years.

Still, Teddy Roosevelt felt proud. He had helped to do something special. He had helped map a river that was about 950 miles long. Today, the River of Doubt is known as the Rio Roosevelt.

Roosevelt's last great adventure had been hard on him.

USE WHAT YOU KNOW

Read and Remember — Choose the Answer

Draw a circle around the correct answer.

1. Who first saw and named the River of Doubt?

   Candido Rondon   Theodore Roosevelt   Kermit Roosevelt

2. Why did the men travel on the River of Doubt?

   to reach Brazil's capital   to map the river   to study snakes

3. What caused the men to roll their canoes and supplies on logs?

   piranha   dense jungle   rapids

4. Where did Kermit Roosevelt get trapped?

   in a cave   in a whirlpool   in his tent

5. What happened to Teddy Roosevelt along the way?

   He became sick.   He got lost.   He was bitten by a snake.

6. What did the River of Doubt become known as?

   Madeira River   Rio Roosevelt   Amazon River

Think About It — Find the Main Ideas

Underline the two most important ideas from the story.

1. Teddy Roosevelt helped explore the River of Doubt.

2. There was an island in the middle of the River of Doubt.

3. Candido Mariano da Silva Rondon was a leader in Brazil's army.

4. Teddy Roosevelt enjoyed listening to bird songs.

5. The trip down the River of Doubt was long and difficult.

6. Some insects in the jungle are poisonous.

Focus on Vocabulary — Crossword Puzzle

Use the clues to complete the puzzle. Choose from the words in dark print.

headwaters	**rapids**	**vegetation**	**poisonous**
piranha	**former**	**whirlpool**	**current**
portage	**burden**		

Across

4. carry over land

6. flow of water in a certain direction

8. small streams that form the beginning of a river

9. small, dangerous fish with sharp teeth

10. causing sickness or death with poison

Down

1. a load that slows a person down

2. plants

3. from the past

5. swirling water

7. fast-moving parts of a river

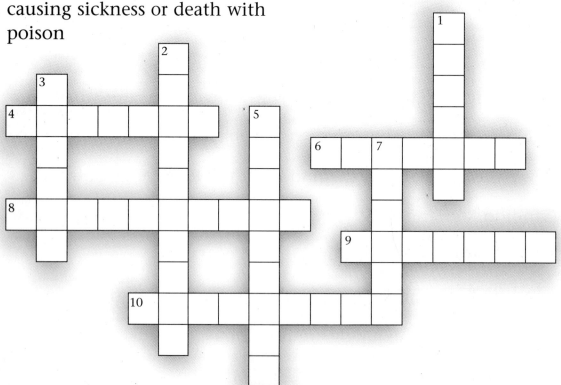

Hemispheres

Earth can be divided into **hemispheres**. The area north of the **equator** is the Northern Hemisphere. The area south of the equator is the Southern Hemisphere. Earth can also be divided into the Eastern Hemisphere and the Western Hemisphere. Study the map below. Write the answer to each question.

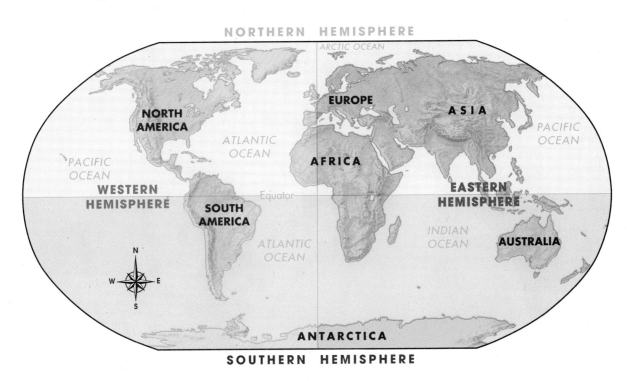

1. Is Antarctica in the Northern or Southern Hemisphere? _____

2. Is the Indian Ocean in the Eastern or Western Hemisphere? __ _____

_____

3. What is the line that separates the Northern and Southern

    Hemispheres called? _____

4. The River of Doubt is in South America. In which three hemispheres is

    South America? _____

5. In which two hemispheres is southern Africa? _____

Jungle Doctor

Albert Schweitzer had a busy life in Germany. He was a minister and a college teacher. He also wrote books and played the organ. But his dream was to serve others. In 1904 he read a story about the need for doctors in Africa. Schweitzer wanted to help. So at the age of 30, he decided to move to West Africa, to the area that is now Gabon. He would start a hospital in the jungle. His life would never be the same.

Starting Over

Schweitzer went back to school for eight years in order to become a doctor. Some of his friends tried to talk him out of it. But he didn't listen. He had always wanted to help people in need. Now he saw a chance to do just that.

Only one person shared Schweitzer's dream with him. Her name was Helene Bresslau. She also went back to school. She studied nursing so she could help Schweitzer in his work. In 1912 Schweitzer and Bresslau got married. A year later, they sailed for Africa with seventy boxes of medicine and equipment. They had no idea what problems they would soon face.

A few weeks later, they arrived at Libreville in Gabon. The couple climbed onto a small boat and headed up the Ogooué River. The thick, green African jungle came right up to the riverb Hundreds of birds sang out. Butterflies f¹ Crocodiles rested in the mud. Monke as they swung from tree to tree.

As the only doctor for miles, Schweitzer was very busy.

Life in the Jungle

The Schweitzers' new home in Gabon was very hot. Gabon is right on the **equator**. So the sun shone straight down on them. The Schweitzers were warned never to go outside without a hat to shade them. Also, the air was so **humid** that their clothes became wet. Mosquitoes covered them with bites.

Still, the Schweitzers felt happy when they got to their new home. It was at a **mission** on an island named Lambaréné. The island was a perfect spot. It was in the middle of the Ogooué River. That made it easy for people to reach by canoe. Schweitzer had to be easy to reach. He was the only doctor for many miles around.

Word of the new doctor spread fast among the area's Africans. Each day, canoes loaded with sick people came to the island. Schweitzer had no place to put these people. So he saw **patients** out in the open air. When it rained, he had to rush to get his supplies under cover before they were ruined.

Clearly, Schweitzer needed a shelter. But he couldn't build one by himself. The men of the area were away, working. Schweitzer searched around the area. Finally, he found an old, empty chicken **coop**. It was very dirty. But he and Helene washed and swept the floor. They painted the walls. They fixed a hole in the roof. At last, Schweitzer had made his own small hospital.

Serving Others

Schweitzer could not **afford** to waste anything. He had to wash and use bandages again and again. He needed tin boxes and glass bottles for his medicines. This was the only way to protect them from the jungle heat. Sometimes his patients did not return the **containers**. So Schweitzer was always looking for more. Every time he wrote his friends in Europe, he asked them to send empty boxes and bottles.

Schweitzer had to deal with all kinds of diseases. Many of them were unknown in Europe. Some were **contagious** and spread easily from one person to another. So Schweitzer had to be very careful. He also had to care for patients with open cuts. Often, these cuts had been caused by crocodile or leopard attacks.

Schweitzer and a helper work with one of the patients.

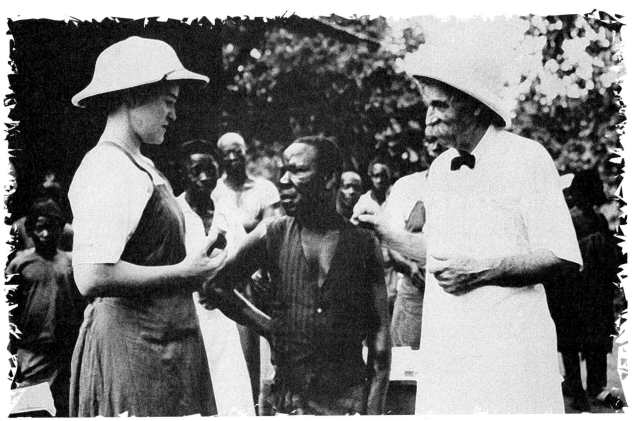

Many of his patients got well. But many others didn't. Yet Schweitzer never thought about giving up. Even with the problems, he kept going. He wrote that the bad things were nothing next to "the joy of being here, working, helping." His wife Helene offered him much support. She worked hard by his side.

Word of Schweitzer's work spread. People around the world sent money to help him. Slowly, Schweitzer's working **conditions** got better. He used some of the money to build a real hospital. Schweitzer made a few trips back to Europe. But he spent most of his life serving the people of Gabon.

In 1953 Albert Schweitzer was awarded the Nobel Peace Prize. The prize was given to honor his work in the jungle. In 1965, at the age of 90, he died. During his last sixty years, Schweitzer never forgot his dream as a young man—to serve others.

In 1953 Schweitzer received the Nobel Peace Prize for his work.

Read and Remember — Check the Events

Place a check in front of the three sentences that tell what happened in the story.

_____ **1.** Albert Schweitzer left Africa to become a doctor.

_____ **2.** The people of Gabon did not trust Albert Schweitzer.

_____ **3.** Schweitzer and his wife Helene set up a hospital in the jungle.

_____ **4.** The Schweitzers settled on an island in the Ogooué River.

_____ **5.** Dr. Schweitzer left Africa when he became too sick to work.

_____ **6.** For a while, Schweitzer worked out of an old chicken coop.

Write About It

Imagine you were one of the people deciding who should win the Nobel Peace Prize. Write a short paragraph describing why Albert Schweitzer deserved to win this great honor.

Focus on Vocabulary — Finish Up

Choose the correct word in dark print to complete each sentence.

equator	**contagious**	**humid**	**riverbanks**
afford	**mission**	**conditions**	**patients**
coop	**containers**		

1. _____ are the ground at the edges of rivers.

2. A place set up in another land to teach people a religion is a

   _____.

3. The imaginary line around Earth's center is the _____.

4. If a disease can be spread from person to person, it is

   _____.

5. A building where small animals are kept is a _____.

6. Sick people who visit a doctor are _____.

7. When the air is damp, it is _____.

8. Your pay, work area, and job hours are part of your working

   _____.

9. Boxes, jars, and bottles are types of _____.

10. To _____ is to be able to pay for, use, or be without.

Map Keys

Maps use different symbols or colors. A **map key** tells what the symbols or colors mean. This map shows the African nation of Gabon, where Dr. Albert Schweitzer worked. Study the map and the map key. Write the answer to each question below.

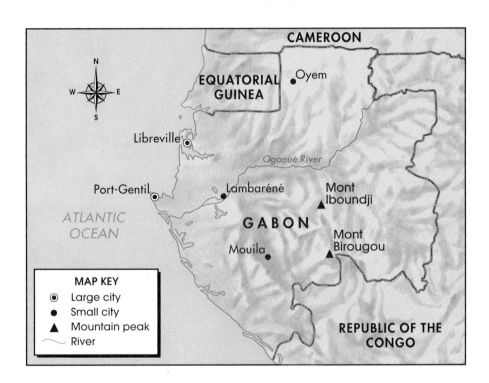

1. Draw the symbol for mountain peak. _____

2. Is the symbol for rain forest shown on the map key? _____

3. Is Libreville a large city or a small city? _____

4. What river is shown on the map? _____

5. What three small cities are shown on the map? _____

_____

6. How many mountain peaks are shown on the map? _____

Across Africa

Delia Akeley had traveled all over East Africa, gathering examples of wildlife with her husband. They had climbed to the top of Mount Kenya. They had stood on the shores of the Tana River. They had visited the great Athi **plains**. Years later, she and her husband divorced. Then in 1924, Delia Akeley left New York and returned to Africa alone. She planned to study some African **customs**. In doing so, she would travel across the whole continent.

Into the Jungle

Akeley began her journey at the **mouth** of the Tana River in Kenya in East Africa. There a man tried to talk her out of her trip. He told her that **nomads** wandered freely in some parts of Africa. Some of them were dangerous. He warned her that she might be attacked. Akeley did not listen to the man. She just went ahead with her plans.

Akeley hired **porters** to carry her bags. She got donkeys for them to ride. She didn't get a donkey for herself, though. She wanted to walk. That turned out to be a mistake. The heat soon tired her out. Her feet became very sore. She had to send a porter back to get one more donkey for her to ride.

After a few days, Akeley decided to travel on the Tana River. She traded the donkeys for canoes from **local** Africans. But the canoes they gave her had holes that had to be patched. Also, they tipped over easily. That scared Akeley. The river was filled with dangerous crocodiles and huge hippos. What if she ended up in the water? Luckily, her porters knew how to handle the canoes.

The sights and sounds of river life amazed Akeley. She wrote, "The brighter and hotter grew the sun, the **livelier** and busier became the life along the river." All kinds of birds flew around the canoes. Many times, Akeley could hear monkeys chattering in the tall trees of the jungle.

On to the Congo

Soon, the food Akeley had bought on the coast made her very sick. She couldn't move. She later said she was "sick to death for days." At last, she was well enough to get moving again.

After ten weeks on the river, Akeley's group reached the hot Somali Desert. Akeley bought some camels for them to ride across the desert. The desert was not a friendly place. Local Africans often attacked **foreigners**. Akeley traveled at night. It was safer and cooler then. Luckily, no one bothered her.

Akeley stands with one of her porters.

A tent kept Akeley out of the sun when she stopped to rest.

After crossing the desert, Akeley headed west to the vast forests of the Belgian Congo. Today, the area is known as the Democratic Republic of the Congo. There Akeley found "rest houses" built just for travelers. But these houses were very dirty. They were filled with snakes and bats. They had holes in the roofs. Akeley hated them. "I could see the fleas jumping on my shirt," she wrote. "They **swarmed** over my hands and face."

Akeley did not keep track of the route she took through the steamy and dangerous Congo. She tried to take notes at night. But it was too hard for her to write. Her light attracted mosquitoes, which would swarm all around her. Akeley kept her skin covered, but they still bothered her.

Life with the Pygmies

Akeley wanted to study the customs of an African tribe of Pygmies. Their villages were so deep in the jungle that there was no trail leading to them. Akeley climbed over big roots and cut her way through thorny vines to get there. The heat of the jungle was fierce. Akeley said she was "wet to the skin, almost as soon as we started."

Delia Akeley

At last, she reached a small Pygmy village. It had only 20 or 30 people. All of them carried weapons. Akeley walked toward the leader. She wasn't sure if he would be angry. Part of her wanted to turn and run away. But she didn't. It turned out that the Pygmies were quite friendly. The leader offered her a drink. He drank first to prove it was safe.

Akeley lived in the Pygmy village for months. She studied the Pygmies' way of life by joining them each day. She played games with them. She helped with their work. She hunted an elephant with them. Akeley even learned to eat what they ate. This meant everything from rats to leaves to caterpillars.

Finally, Akeley left the Pygmies and headed west again. She soon faced other challenges. She came down with terrible fevers. She **braved** rainstorms and slept in mud. Bugs of all kinds bit her. She lost thirty pounds.

Yet on September 3, 1925, Delia Akeley reached the west coast of Africa. It had taken her almost 11 months to cross the continent. But she had made it. Along the way, she had learned to live with her fears. "I'm always frightened in the jungle," she said. "But I love it."

Akeley met many different people during her jungle travels.

USE WHAT YOU KNOW

Read and Remember — Finish the Sentence

Circle the best ending for each sentence.

1. Delia Akeley began her African journey in 1924 in _____.

Kenya   a Pygmy village   South Africa

2. For the first part of the journey, Akeley rode on _____.

a camel   a donkey   an elephant

3. Akeley became ill from _____.

food she had bought   a monkey bite   thirst

4. In the Belgian Congo, Akeley sometimes slept in _____.

boats   rest houses   trees

5. Akeley studied the Pygmies' way of life _____.

by joining them   while staying out of sight   from books

6. After Akeley left the Pygmy village, she headed _____.

west   to the Somali Desert   to the Indian Ocean

Think About It — Fact or Opinion

A **fact** is a true statement. An **opinion** is a statement that tells what a person thinks. Write **F** beside each statement that is a fact. Write **O** beside each statement that is an opinion.

_____ **1.** A man tried to talk Akeley out of traveling across Africa.

_____ **2.** Akeley worried that her canoe might tip over.

_____ **3.** The crocodile is the scariest animal in Africa.

_____ **4.** Akeley should have kept better track of the route she traveled.

_____ **5.** The Pygmies lived deep in the jungle.

_____ **6.** Akeley's route was too dangerous.

Focus on Vocabulary — Make a Word

Choose a word in dark print to complete each sentence. Write the letters of the word on the blanks. When you are finished, the letters in the circles will tell you where Akeley ended her journey.

mouth	**nomads**	**customs**	**foreigners**
swarmed	**local**	**plains**	**braved**
livelier	**porters**		

1. Many bugs _____ over Akeley in the jungle.
   ○ _ _ _ _ _ _ _

2. Akeley _____ rainstorms and other challenges.
   ○ _ _ _ _ _ _

3. Akeley studied Pygmy _____, including how they worked.
   ○ _ _ _ _ _ _ _

4. The _____ of the Tana River is in Kenya.
   ○ _ _ _ _ _

5. _____ wandered through parts of Africa.
   ○ _ _ _ _ _ _

6. _____ traveling in the desert were sometimes attacked.
   ○ _ _ _ _ _ _ _ _ _

7. Akeley hired _____ to carry her bags.
   ○ _ _ _ _ _ _ _

8. Life along the river became _____ in the hot sun.
   ○ _ _ _ _ _ _ _

9. Akeley got canoes from _____ Africans who lived nearby.
   ○ _ _ _ _ _

10. Akeley visited the great Athi _____.
    ○ _ _ _ _ _ _

Latitude and Longitude

You can find places on globes and maps by using lines. Lines that run east to west are lines of **latitude**. Lines that run north to south are lines of **longitude**. All the lines are measured using **degrees**, or °. Much of Delia Akeley's travels was along the equator, the 0° latitude. Study the map. Circle the answer that best completes each sentence below.

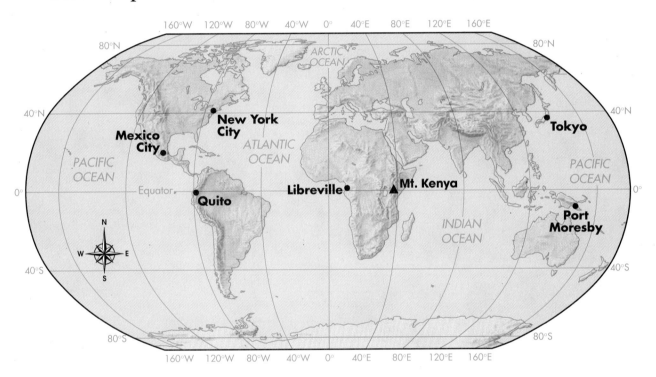

1. What is the latitude of New York City?

41°N   41°W   80°N

2. What is the longitude of Mexico City?

99°W   20°S   20°W

3. Which place has a latitude of 9°S?

Port Moresby   Mexico City   Tokyo

4. Which place on the equator has a longitude of 37°E?

Quito   Libreville   Mount Kenya

Plane Crash in the Jungle

argaret Hastings, a soldier in the United States Army, couldn't wait to see Hidden Valley. It was tucked into the mountains of New Guinea, an island in the Pacific Ocean. Few foreigners had ever seen the **remote** valley. So Hastings was excited to join 23 other soldiers on a flight over the area. The group left on May 13, 1945. They planned to fly over the valley and then return to **base**. Sadly, it would be the last trip most of them ever took.

Into Hidden Valley

When Hastings climbed onto the plane, she took a seat up front. But she wanted a better view of the jungle-covered area. So she moved to a window seat in the back. That move saved her life.

When the plane reached Hidden Valley, the pilot dropped to a low **altitude**. He flew just 300 feet above the ground. That way everyone could see the beautiful green jungle below. But suddenly, something went wrong. The plane hit the side of a mountain. Nineteen soldiers died in the crash. They all had been sitting in the front of the plane.

Hastings lived through the crash. She crawled out of the wrecked plane, which was in flames. But her legs were very burned, and her face was **blistered**. Some of her hair was burned off. Three other soldiers were also badly hurt in the plane crash. They were Kenneth Decker, Eleanor Hanna, and Laura Besley. Only one other soldier, John McCollom, had no **injuries**.

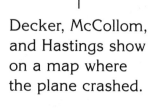

Decker, McCollom, and Hastings show on a map where the plane crashed.

As night came over the jungle, the five **survivors** sat shivering near the crashed plane. The mountain air was cold. Rain fell, making the group even colder. By morning, Eleanor Hanna was dead.

That day, a search plane flew over Hidden Valley. McCollom tried to signal it with a mirror. But it was no use. No pilot could see through the thick tangle of trees. The soldiers had no choice. They would have to walk until they found a **clearing** in the dense jungle.

The Long Walk

The group agreed to begin walking the next morning. But first, they had to get through another night. Laura Besley didn't make it. She died that evening. The remaining three soldiers sat in the jungle, thinking of their dead friends. "No night will ever again be as long as that one," Hastings later said.

When morning finally came, Hastings, McCollom, and Decker headed down the mountain. They had no trail to follow. They just started walking through the jungle. Branches kept catching Hastings's long hair. So she told McCollom to cut it off. Using a tiny knife, he cut off all but an inch or two.

On and on they went. It rained often and hard. They came to a mountain stream and began to follow it. Soon they reached a big waterfall. There was no easy way to get past it. So they used a tree vine to swing over the waterfall.

After hours of walking, Hastings was ready to give up. Her blistered feet and burned legs had become **infected**. It hurt her to walk. Yet she knew she had no choice. Somehow she kept going.

Finally, they came to a small clearing. They waited there until another search plane flew over. When they saw the plane, they quickly spread out some large yellow sheets they had been carrying.

The plane circled around. The pilot dipped the plane's wings to show he had seen them. The three survivors leaped with joy. "We jumped up and down," said Hastings. "We screamed and waved our arms."

Rescued

The clearing was not big enough for the plane to land. A larger space would have to be cut out of the jungle. That would take weeks. Workers would have

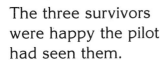

The three survivors were happy the pilot had seen them.

to be sent in by **parachute**. In the meantime, planes would drop some supplies and medicine. Other than that, the three soldiers were still on their own.

Then, as the survivors stood in the clearing, a group of **native** people appeared. The natives and the soldiers smiled at each other. The soldiers offered gifts of hard candy and a mirror. Later, the natives brought food.

Almost a week later, two medical soldiers dropped by parachute into the jungle. They helped take care of the infected wounds that Decker and Hastings had. Meanwhile, the five soldiers became good friends with the natives. They even visited the natives' village.

Finally, rescue workers arrived. A bigger clearing had been cut. But it was 45 miles away. So Hastings, Decker, and McCollom set out through the jungle once again, following the other soldiers.

When they reached the new clearing, a plane picked them up and flew them back to the Army base. They had spent 47 days in the jungle. Hastings would miss the many kind natives she had come to know. But back on the base, her thoughts were on the 21 soldiers that were buried in the jungles of Hidden Valley.

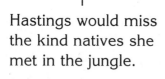

Hastings would miss the kind natives she met in the jungle.

Read and Remember — Choose the Answer

Draw a circle around the correct answer.

1. Where did the plane crash?

near Hidden Valley   in a river   in a clearing

2. How many soldiers died from the plane crash?

three   five   twenty-one

3. How did the soldiers first try to signal the search plane?

with a fire   with a mirror   by waving a cloth

4. How did the search plane's pilot show that he saw the soldiers?

He dropped ropes.   He dipped the wings.   He waved.

5. What prevented the plane from landing right away?

dense trees   heavy rain   fog

6. What did the native people give to the group?

knives   canoes   food

Write About It

Imagine you were one of the native people of New Guinea in 1945. Write three questions you would want to ask the soldiers you met.

1. _____

_____

2. _____

_____

3. _____

_____

Focus on Vocabulary — Find the Meaning

Read each sentence. Circle the best meaning for the word in dark print.

1. The plane flew over the **remote** Hidden Valley.

far away   beautiful   wide

2. The soldiers planned to return to the **base** after the flight.

Army station   center of the jungle   dining hall

3. The plane dropped to a low **altitude**.

height above the ground   radio channel   patch of trees

4. Margaret Hastings's face was **blistered**.

cut   smooth   covered with small bubbles

5. John McCollom had no **injuries**.

ropes   maps   wounds

6. Margaret Hastings was one of the **survivors**.

people who lived   leaders   soldiers

7. The three soldiers looked for a **clearing** in the dense jungle.

village   pond   open area

8. Margaret Hastings's feet became **infected**.

very cold   diseased   tired

9. Workers were sent in by **parachute** to help the soldiers.

river   cloth used to slow a person in air   airplane

10. A group of **native** people appeared.

angry   helpful   originally living there

Countries

Some maps give information about countries. Thin lines are used to show the **borders** between countries. The map key explains what symbols are used on the map. This map shows Indonesia and nearby countries. Study the map and the map key. Write the answer to each question.

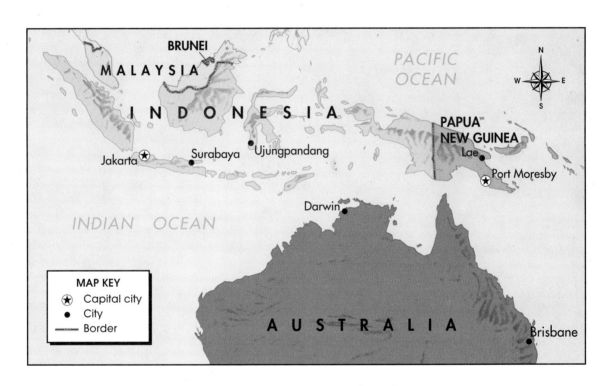

1. What is the capital city of Papua New Guinea? _____

2. What cities in Australia are shown on the map? _____

3. Of which country is Jakarta the capital city? _____

4. Which country shares a border with Papua New Guinea? _____

5. Which country shares a border with Brunei? _____

6. In which country is the city Lae? _____

Saving the Mountain Gorillas

Dian Fossey said, "I had this great **urge,** this need to go to Africa. I had it the day I was born." In 1963 Fossey finally made it. She went to Africa for a seven-week visit to see mountain gorillas. These gorillas live only in the jungle-covered Virunga Mountains of East Africa. Fossey was amazed by the gorillas. She wanted to learn more about them. Three years later, she returned to the Virungas. This time she came to stay.

Getting Close

There were many reasons why Dian Fossey wanted to study mountain gorillas. The animals had only been discovered in 1902. Yet by the 1960s, their numbers were getting smaller as people took their land or killed them. They were in danger of becoming **extinct**. No one knew much about them. Fossey wanted to study them before it was too late.

Fossey wanted to see how the gorillas lived in their natural **habitat** of the rain forest. What did they eat? How did they act toward one another?

Getting answers to these questions wouldn't be easy. Mountain gorillas were shy. They **avoided** people. Also, they lived in the cold, misty jungles of the Virungas. The gorillas' **range** crossed into the countries of Rwanda, Uganda, and the Democratic Republic of the Congo. If Fossey was going to study the mountain gorillas, she would have to live up there with them.

When Fossey first moved into the jungle, she stayed far away from the gorillas. She didn't want to frighten

The mountain gorillas live in the misty jungles of the Virungas.

them. After a few weeks, she began to copy their actions from a distance. In this way, she hoped they would accept her. She saw them beat their chests. So she made the same sound by slapping her hands on her legs. "I thought I was very clever," Fossey later said. But it was the wrong signal. A gorilla beats its chest to sound an alarm.

Fossey learned from her mistake. In time, she discovered what she should do. She ate the same food as the gorillas. She groomed herself the same way they did. She walked like them. She made the same soft sounds. It worked. After a few months, the gorillas accepted her. Then Fossey could study them up close.

Living with Gorillas

Fossey learned that mountain gorillas eat plants, not meat. They sleep in nests on the ground. Every day they travel about a quarter of a mile through thick, cool forests.

Fossey also found that they aren't fierce like many people believe. Most of the time they are gentle. They take care of each other. They walk only as fast as the slowest one. Mountain gorillas don't look for a fight.

But if someone in their family is attacked, they will fight to the death.

Fossey grew to love the gorillas. She gave them all names. Often she cuddled up with these 400-pound creatures. The gorillas even let her play with their babies. Her favorite was a baby she called Digit.

Living with the mountain gorillas changed Fossey's life. "I have no husband, children," she said. "It's just me and the gorillas." In fact, she grew to like them better than people. "I have no friends," she said. "The more that you learn about the **dignity** of the gorilla, the more you want to avoid people."

Troubles in the Jungle

She shared her **research** with the world and wrote a book about the "gentle giants." Even though she loved her work, Dian Fossey had trouble living in the jungle. The thin air and damp **climate** made her sick. She ate poorly. By 1985 she was worn out. She had trouble breathing. Yet she refused to leave the gorillas.

Once the gorillas accepted Fossey, she began to study them up close.

Dian Fossey

Meanwhile, Fossey had made many human enemies. She fought with African **officials**. She fought with visitors who came to see the gorillas. She even fought with college students who came to study with her.

Most of all, she fought with local hunters. They often came up into the Virungas. They set wire traps to catch small animals. But sometimes gorillas got caught instead. Some gorillas lost a finger or hand in the traps. Others died. One who died was Digit.

Fossey was **heartbroken** each time a gorilla was killed. She buried each one carefully. Meanwhile, she grew angry with the hunters. She broke their traps. Whenever she came upon hunters, she found ways to take away their weapons.

Fossey knew the hunters hated her. She began sleeping with a gun next to her. But that wasn't enough to keep her safe. On December 27, 1985, someone broke into Fossey's cabin and killed her. No one ever found out who did it.

Dian Fossey was buried next to her gorilla friends. Her life was over, but the work she did lived on. Thanks to her, people knew a lot about the mountain gorillas. People around the world began working to save these beautiful jungle animals.

In 1985 someone broke into Fossey's cabin and killed her.

Read and Remember — Check the Events

Place a check in front of the three sentences that tell what happened in the story.

_____ **1.** By the 1960s the number of mountain gorillas had increased.

_____ **2.** Dian Fossey ate the same foods as the gorillas.

_____ **3.** Fossey enjoyed the dry climate of the Virunga Mountains.

_____ **4.** Digit was killed by a hunter's trap.

_____ **5.** The mountain gorillas did not let Fossey near their babies.

_____ **6.** Fossey was killed by one of her enemies.

Think About It — Cause and Effect

A **cause** is something that makes something else happen. What happens is called the **effect**. Match each cause with an effect. Write the letter on the correct blank. The first one is done for you.

Cause	Effect
1. Dian Fossey wanted to study mountain gorillas, so __c__	**a.** she gave them time to get used to her.
2. Fossey didn't want to scare the gorillas, so _____	**b.** some gorillas lost a finger or died.
3. Fossey copied the gorillas' actions, so _____	**c.** she moved to the Virunga Mountains.
4. Animal traps sometimes caught gorillas, so _____	**d.** people are working to save the gentle giants.
5. The mountain gorillas were almost extinct, so _____	**e.** the gorillas began to accept her.

USE WHAT YOU KNOW

Focus on Vocabulary — Finish the Paragraphs

Use the words in dark print to complete the paragraphs. Reread the paragraphs to be sure they make sense.

extinct	**avoided**	**climate**	**officials**
heartbroken	**dignity**	**habitat**	**range**
research	**urge**		

Dian Fossey had a strong (1)_____, or want, to visit Africa. There, she saw some mountain gorillas. These animals were in danger of dying out, or becoming (2)_____. Fossey wanted to study them in their natural (3)_____ of the rain forest. Their (4)_____ crossed into three countries of Africa. The area's (5)_____ was damp and cold.

The gorillas were shy and (6)_____ people, but Fossey came to know them well. In fact, she gave them all names. She thought that they had more (7)_____ than people do. She felt very (8)_____ when some were killed by hunters' traps.

Fossey made many enemies. Some of them were hunters. Others were government (9)_____. Then in 1985, someone killed her. Fossey's life had ended, but her work continued. People are still trying to save the mountain gorillas, thanks to Dian Fossey and her (10)_____.

Elevation

An area of land can have different **elevations**, or heights. Some areas have low plains. Other areas have tall mountains, such as the Virungas in East Africa. The map below uses colors to show different elevations in East Africa. The map key shows which color is used for certain heights. Study the map and the map key. Circle the best answer to each question.

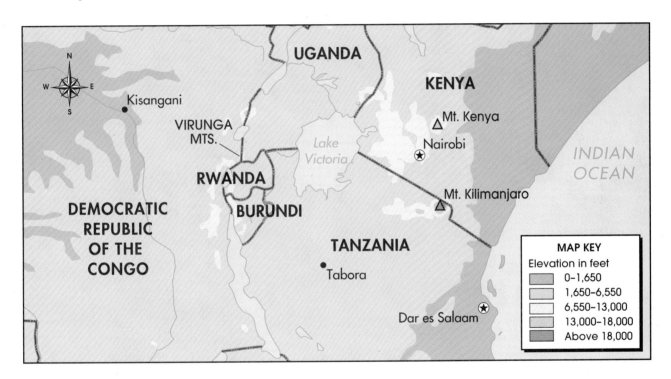

1. Which color shows the lowest land elevation?

   dark orange   dark green   yellow

2. What is the elevation of Kisangani?

   0–1,650 feet   1,650–6,550 feet   6,550–13,000 feet

3. Which city has the lowest elevation?

   Dar es Salaam   Nairobi   Tabora

4. What is the elevation of Mount Kilimanjaro?

   1,650–6,550 feet   6,550–13,000 feet   above 18,000 feet

28 Years in the Jungle

Shoichi Yokoi did not want to be captured. During World War II, the Japanese soldier had been sent to Guam, an island in the Pacific Ocean. On July 21, 1944, the United States Army landed at Guam to gain control of the island from the Japanese. A fierce battle broke out. Most of Yokoi's group were killed. But Yokoi fled into the jungles of southern Guam. The war ended in 1945. But Yokoi didn't come out of the jungle for 28 years.

Into the Jungle

Before the war, Shoichi Yokoi had been a **tailor** in a small town in Japan. He had a girlfriend and was thinking about getting married. But then World War II began. In 1941 Japan went to war against the United States. Yokoi was ordered to join the Japanese army. In 1944 he was sent to Guam. He had been there four months when the Americans arrived.

When Yokoi ran into the Guam jungle, nine other soldiers went with him. They knew that they couldn't stay together. A group that big soon would be caught. So they split up. Most of the men were soon captured or died in the jungle.

Yokoi and two other soldiers ended up near the Talofofo River. There the jungle was dense, and the **tropical** air was hot and humid. Mosquitoes buzzed everywhere. Snakes slithered between the trees. Frogs and rats crawled along the wet ground.

The three men hid in the **bamboo**. Each day they went looking for food. But there wasn't much to be found. The men ate coconuts. They also ate frogs and snails. They caught shrimp and eels from the nearby river. Even so, there wasn't enough food to keep them all alive. After a few months, the other two men moved off to another part of the jungle. Yokoi stayed near the Talofofo River.

One day, Yokoi found an old newspaper someone had dropped. It told him that World War II was over. The United States and its **allies** had won. Yokoi found the newspaper in 1946, a year after the war had ended.

Even though the war was over, Yokoi did not want to come out of hiding. He was afraid the American soldiers would kill him. Besides, he had been taught that it was better to die than to **surrender**.

An Underground Cave

Yokoi decided to stay in the jungle. He moved deep into a bamboo **grove**. There, on the **slope** of a hill, he dug an underground cave in which to live. Every day he scooped away a little dirt. He carried the dirt

Yokoi hid in the jungle to avoid capture by the American soldiers.

Yokoi's cave was so small that he had to crouch inside.

off by hand and spread it around in a nearby field. That way no one would notice it.

The entrance to the cave was very narrow. It went down about eight feet. Yokoi built a ladder to climb in and out. At the bottom, he dug a ten-foot cave. The cave was about four feet high. So whenever Yokoi was in it, he had to crouch.

At the far end of the cave, Yokoi dug an air hole to help him breathe. He lit small fires in the cave to cook his food. To light fires, he rubbed sticks together until they made a spark. Later, he took **fiber** from coconuts and made ropes that burned slowly for hours. That allowed him to keep a fire going. In time, the **soot** from his fire covered everything inside the cave.

Yokoi wore his one set of clothes until they fell apart. Then he used his skill as a tailor to make new ones. He took fiber from the bark of trees. By weaving it together, he made a kind of cloth. He made needles from old nails and buttons from small pieces of wood. He even made shoes out of coconut shells.

Yokoi collected rainwater for drinking. He also made daily trips to the river. He would sneak there each morning before dawn and each night after dark. Quietly, he would check his homemade shrimp traps. Then he would return to his underground cave.

Found At Last

As the years passed, Yokoi sometimes would visit the two soldiers with whom he had lived in the jungle for a few months. But one day in 1964, he discovered that his two friends had died, probably from their poor **diet**. Yokoi was completely alone.

For eight more years, Yokoi lived in the jungles of Guam. Then, on the night of January 24, 1972, he went to check his shrimp traps. Suddenly, he was spotted by two fishermen. This time there was no escape. The men took him to the police. There, he told his story.

A few days later, Yokoi was sent home to Japan. He was given a hero's welcome. But Yokoi himself had mixed feelings. "It is a terrible shame for me," he said. "I came back, still alive, without having won the war." He wondered, "Maybe I should have stayed in my cave and died." But another part of Yokoi felt differently. When he had been out of the jungle for just two days, he announced, "I'm glad that I'm alive."

Shoichi Yokoi was given a hero's welcome.

Read and Remember — Finish the Sentence

 **Circle the best ending for each sentence.**

1. Shoichi Yokoi was a soldier from _____.

the United States   Japan   Guam

2. Yokoi spent many years living in _____.

an underground cave   a tree   a small village in Guam

3. Yokoi made cloth from _____.

coconuts   tree bark   shrimp

4. When Yokoi found out that World War II had ended, he _____.

continued to hide   looked for help   went to see the Americans

5. Yokoi was finally spotted by two _____.

doctors   fishermen   American soldiers

6. People in Japan gave Yokoi _____.

a hero's welcome   a house in Guam   new shrimp traps

Write About It

Imagine you were a newspaper reporter in the 1970s. You are going to interview Shoichi Yokoi about his 28 years in the jungle. Write three questions you would like to ask him.

1. _____

_____

2. _____

_____

3. _____

_____

USE WHAT YOU KNOW

Focus on Vocabulary — Match Up

Match each word with its meaning. Write the correct letter on the blank.

_____ 1. tailor

_____ 2. bamboo

_____ 3. diet

_____ 4. fiber

_____ 5. grove

_____ 6. allies

_____ 7. tropical

_____ 8. surrender

_____ 9. soot

_____ 10. slope

a. give up

b. countries that unite to do something

c. usual food and drink

d. powder made when a fire burns

e. group of trees

f. person who makes clothes

g. tall grass that looks like tubes of wood

h. thread-like material from plants and trees

i. ground that slants

j. of hot, wet areas near the equator

Distance Scale

On a map, use a **distance scale** to find the distance between two places. On this map of Guam, the distance scale shows that 1 inch of the map stands for 10 miles of land. Use a ruler to measure the distances on the map. Circle the correct answer to each question.

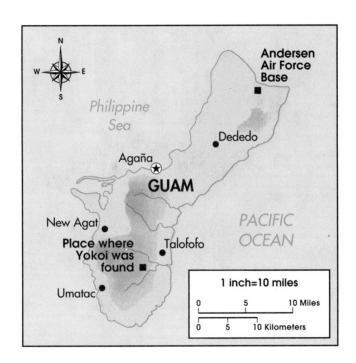

1. On the map, how many inches are between Agaña and the place where Yokoi was found?

   $\frac{1}{2}$ inch   2 inches   1 inch

2. What is the actual distance between Agaña and Yokoi's spot?

   20 miles   10 miles   5 miles

3. What is the actual distance between Umatac and the Air Force base?

   26 miles   15 miles   20 miles

4. Which place is about 6 miles from where Yokoi was found?

   Talofofo   Dededo   New Agat

Rain Forest Hero

Chico Mendes had many enemies. Some even wanted him dead. In May of 1988, Mendes got an unsigned note saying that he would soon be killed. Mendes's friends begged him to go into hiding. But Mendes refused to leave Xapuri, his village in the rain forest of Brazil in South America. "I would be a **coward** to do this," he told his friends. "There's something inside me that cannot leave here." That was a brave decision. But it was one that would cost him his life.

The Burning Season

Mendes's home was in the beautiful Amazon rain forest. It is hot and wet there all year long. Countless **species** of plants and animals live in the steamy jungle. Most of the animals live in the green roof of treetops, called the **canopy**. Many of these animals rarely, if ever, touch the ground. Some species of the rain forest's plants are the sources of medicine. Many trees provide fruit, nuts, and sap that help forest people earn a living.

Mendes was a rubber tree **tapper** in the western part of the Amazon rain forest. He learned the job as a young boy. Tappers make small cuts in rubber trees. This allows **sap** to run out. The sap is then used to make rubber. Since the cutting does not hurt the trees, each tree can be used over and over again. But tapping trees does not pay much money. Mendes and his family were very poor.

Many other people in Brazil's jungles were tree tappers. But they were not the only ones living in the

A tree tapper makes small cuts in a rubber tree to make sap run out.

jungles. Cattle ranchers also lived there. They needed open spaces for their cattle. So they wanted to get rid of the trees. Each year these ranchers cut or burned thousands of **acres** of trees. This was called the "burning season."

For a while, it looked like nothing could stop the ranchers. They destroyed more and more of Brazil's rain forest. In addition, other people began moving in. New roads were laid. Houses and buildings were put up. All this meant that more of the rain forest was cut down. In just 20 years, more than 230,000 square miles of trees were burned or cut down. That's more land than California and Florida put together.

Fighting Back

Chico Mendes saw what the ranchers were doing. In 1977 Mendes began to fight back. He formed a **union** of tree tappers. It was called the Rural Workers Union. The union tried to get higher prices for tree sap. More importantly, it worked to save the rain forest from the ranchers.

As the trees are destroyed by ranchers, millions of animals and other plants die. Such **deforestation** can cause entire species to become extinct. In addition, many forest people lose their homes and their ways of life. Tree tappers lose their jobs, too. Mendes knew he had to find a way to stop the ranchers.

Mendes told his group to fight peacefully. He got them to stand in front of the bulldozers. This often worked. The drivers didn't want to run people down. So they turned off their engines. In this way, Mendes saved about 3 million acres of the Amazon rain forest.

News of Mendes's cause soon spread beyond Brazil. Many people around the world agreed with him. They saw the danger of cutting down the trees, too. More people began to help Mendes in his fight.

At last, in 1988 Brazil's leaders stepped in. They selected 5 million acres of land. They said that no one was allowed to cut the trees within those **boundaries**. It wasn't much compared to the amount of forest being destroyed, but at least some land was saved.

The ranchers, however, continued to hate Mendes. They saw him as a **threat** to their way of life. Some of them offered him money to go away. But Mendes refused. That made the ranchers even more angry.

Mendes wanted the "burning season" to end.

Paying the Price

When Mendes got the unsigned death threat, he knew it was no joke. Other tree tappers had already been killed. In December of 1988, Mendes turned 44 years old. That night he went out with his wife, Ilzamar. He took her in his arms. "This will probably be my last birthday with you," he told her.

One week later, Mendes went to take a shower before dinner. The shower was outside the house. Just as he opened the back door to step outside, someone opened fire. Mendes fell backwards. "They got me!" he said, falling dead on the kitchen floor.

After his death, Mendes became even more famous. His life story was turned into a movie. People wrote books about him. His ideas grew more popular. People worked harder to save the jungles of Brazil. For a few years, the cutting and burning of trees slowed down. Then the rate of cutting went up again. So the fight to save this beautiful and important rain forest goes on even today.

Chico Mendes was truly a rain forest hero.

USE WHAT YOU KNOW

Read and Remember — Choose the Answer

Draw a circle around the correct answer.

1. Where was Xapuri, Chico Mendes's village?

   India   Colombia   Brazil

2. What did cattle ranchers need for their cattle?

   quieter forests   more water   open spaces

3. What name was given to the cutting and burning of trees?

   the burning season   land of fire   tree tapping

4. Who were angry at Chico Mendes?

   forest people   tree tappers   ranchers

5. How did Mendes want his people to fight?

   with bulldozers   with weapons   peacefully

6. What happened to Chico Mendes?

   He was shot to death.   He became president.   He fled.

Think About It — Find the Main Ideas

Underline the two most important ideas from the story.

1. Some of Chico Mendes's friends lived in the town of Xapuri.

2. Mendes fought to help protect the rain forest.

3. In December of 1988, Chico Mendes turned 44 years old.

4. Some rain forest plants are used to make medicine.

5. Mendes didn't want ranchers to cut down more trees.

6. Chico Mendes was married.

USE WHAT YOU KNOW

Focus on Vocabulary — Find the Meaning

Read each sentence. Circle the best meaning for the word in dark print.

1. Chico Mendes didn't want to be a **coward**.

    rancher   leader   frightened person

2. There are many **species** of plants in the rain forest.

    kinds   colors   eaters

3. Many animals live in the **canopy** of the rain forest.

    river   covering of treetops   tangle of vines

4. Mendes was a tree **tapper**.

    owner   hater   person who draws liquid

5. There is **sap** in each tree.

    liquid food   energy   bark

6. The ranchers burned thousands of **acres** of trees.

    different kinds   units of measure for land   seeds

7. Mendes started a **union**.

    new business   farm   group of workers

8. Mendes wanted to stop the **deforestation**.

    fighting   selling of cattle   clearing away of trees

9. No one was allowed to cut trees within the area's **boundaries**.

    ranches   river systems   limits

10. The ranchers felt that Mendes was a **threat** to them.

    friend   danger   boss

USE A MAP

Countries

Some maps give information about countries. Thin lines are used to show the **borders** between countries. The map key explains what symbols are used on the map. This map shows Brazil and nearby countries in South America. Study the map and the map key. Write the answer to each question.

1. What is the capital city of Colombia? _____

2. Which three countries share a border with Suriname? _____

_____

3. Of which country is Fortaleza a city? _____

4. Of which country is Cayenne the capital city? _____

5. Which city is near the border between Brazil and Bolivia? _____

6. Does the Amazon River flow through Peru? _____

The Place of the Dead

On a mountain high in Southeast Asia lies the Place of the Dead. It is a ten-mile area of jungle, waterfalls, and cliffs on Malaysia's Mount Kinabalu. According to **legend,** this jungle area is where spirits of dead people gather. Local villagers won't go near it. But in February of 1994, ten soldiers tried to enter it. It was a trip that almost killed them.

Problems from the Start

The team's journey to the Place of the Dead began on February 21, 1994. British army officer Robert Neill was in charge. Neill knew that the days in the jungle would be hard. He was testing his men to see how tough they were.

His plan was for his men to climb to the **summit** of the 13,432-foot Mount Kinabalu, on the island of Borneo. Then they would enter the Place of the Dead, which is also known as Low's Gully. They would head down the one-mile-deep **ravine** between two walls of rock. At the bottom was a thick jungle floor. No one had ever managed to climb down to it before. Neill hoped his group would be the first. From there, they would cut their way out of the dense, green jungle.

The expedition had trouble from the start. The ten men did not work well as a team. The five strongest soldiers wanted to move quickly. But three other men had trouble carrying their 88-pound packs. Neill tried to keep the group together. Soon, though, he became sick. It was all he could do to take care of himself. He had no strength left to lead the others.

Traveling through the dense, misty jungle was very difficult.

At the top of the mountain, the group split in two. The five strongest men were eager to enter Low's Gully. They took most of the rope, planning to lower themselves down into the ravine. They also took all the big knives with them to cut through the thick jungle at the bottom. They said they would mark the trail as they went. That way the slower soldiers would know where to go.

Five Men Reach Safety

About two weeks later, on March 12, the faster half of the group **staggered** out of the jungle. They were worn out. The trip had been harder than they expected. They had been soaked by rainstorms. One man had fallen sixty feet and hit his head on a rock. The others had to carry him.

Then the men ran out of food. They had trouble finding things to eat in the deep, wet jungle. Most of the plants they saw were poisonous. Most jungle animals stayed out of sight. All the men saw were two snakes the size of pencils. By the time they reached safety, they were very weak with hunger.

But at least these five men were alive. No one knew what had happened to Robert Neill and the four men with him. They might already be dead. If they weren't, they were still somewhere deep in the jungle, in the Place of the Dead.

Quickly, the Malaysian army put together a large **search party**. More than 300 Malaysians began to **hack** their way through the dense jungle plants. Helicopter pilots flew over the mountain. But soon a heavy mist covered the area. The mist made it impossible for the pilots to see below. Day after day, members of the search party found nothing.

Waiting and Hoping

As it turned out, Neill and the four other soldiers were still alive. They were stuck on a **ledge** in Low's Gully. They had climbed part of the way down. But the cliff was too steep for them to keep going. It was also too steep for them to go back up. On both sides of them roared giant waterfalls. One **rescuer** later said the men were trapped "like a spider in the bathtub."

The soldiers took white pebbles and laid them on a huge black rock beside the river. The pebbles spelled the emergency sign "**S.O.S.**" Then the men waited,

The men used pebbles to write S.O.S., so they might be rescued.

hoping for help to come. They tried to make their food last as long as possible. For days, they ate only biscuit crumbs. Then the crumbs ran out. After that, the starving men had only water to keep themselves alive.

Finally, Neill and his men saw the rescue helicopters flying over them. But they realized that the pilots couldn't see them in the mist. The soldiers just kept hoping they'd be found soon.

On March 25, Malaysian helicopter pilot Mohamed Izhar was about to give up searching for the day. Suddenly, he spotted the S.O.S. "I dropped down and saw three men waving and flashing mirrors," he said. At last, after 29 days of being lost, Neill and his men had been located.

The helicopter could not land in the narrow ravine. So food and **stretchers** were lowered down on ropes. The rescuers had to stop when the mist became thick. It took two days to rescue all five men from the ledge. At last, all five soldiers were pulled out. Robert Neill had lost almost thirty pounds. He said, "I came very close to death." He also added, "We will never be the same people ever again."

Robert Neill was glad to be safe at last.

Read and Remember — Check the Events

Place a check in front of the three sentences that tell what happened in the story.

_____ **1.** Robert Neill led a group of soldiers toward Low's Gully.

_____ **2.** The men traded their knives and rope for food.

_____ **3.** Some of the men decided to stay and live in the Place of the Dead.

_____ **4.** Neill and four others ate biscuit crumbs to stay alive.

_____ **5.** A helicopter crashed while trying to rescue the men.

_____ **6.** Malaysians cut through the jungle to rescue Neill's group.

Write About It

Imagine you were one of the men rescued by Mohamed Izhar, the helicopter pilot. Write a letter to him, expressing how you feel.

Dear _____ ,

_____

_____

_____

_____

_____

_____

_____

Focus on Vocabulary — Finish Up

Choose the correct word in dark print to complete each sentence.

ledge	**rescuer**	**S.O.S.**	**search party**
staggered	**ravine**	**hack**	**summit**
stretchers	**legend**		

1. A call for help is an _____.

2. _____ means walked in a shaky way.

3. A story passed down through the years is a _____.

4. To cut with heavy blows is to _____.

5. A person who comes to help someone in trouble is a

   _____.

6. The top of a mountain is the _____.

7. A narrow shelf of rock is a _____.

8. A group who looks for missing people is a _____.

9. A deep, narrow area of land between two walls of rock is a

   _____.

10. Light beds used to carry injured people are _____.

Latitude and Longitude

Lines that run east to west around Earth are lines of **latitude**. Lines that run north to south are lines of **longitude**. All the lines are measured in **degrees**, or °. Latitude and longitude can be used together to show a place's location. For example, Mount Kinabalu in Malaysia is at 6°N, 117°E. The latitude is written first, then the longitude. Study the map below. Circle the answer that best completes each sentence.

1. The city with a longitude of 114°E is _____.

Banjarmasin   Jakarta   Pontianak

2. The city that is on the equator, or 0° latitude, is _____.

Pontianak   Surabaya   Ujungpandang

3. The longitude of Zamboanga is _____.

122°E   125°E   5°N

4. The city at 5°S, 119°E is _____.

Ujungpandang   Zamboanga   Surabaya

Pushed to
the Limit

Sergeant Norman Tillman wanted to be an Army Ranger. These United States soldiers must be ready to fight anywhere. During training, they fight imaginary enemies in jungles, mountains, and deserts. Tillman knew the nine weeks of training would be hard. He would be pushed to his **limit**. But in February of 1995, Tillman began a test in a Florida swamp that would be more than difficult. It would be deadly.

Hanging On

Tillman was 28 years old. He was the oldest **trainee** in his Ranger class. He was strong and fit. He believed he could pass all the tough tests his **instructors** gave him.

During the first part of the training, the soldiers were tested for mountain and desert fighting. By the end of those eight weeks, the trainees were worn out. Many had lost 20 or 30 pounds. In fact, two-thirds of the 334 men had dropped out or had failed a test. Tillman was one of 102 men still in the program.

For those 102 soldiers, the last week of training would be in the swamp for the jungle test. During that time, the soldiers would spend a lot of time in very cold water.

Sergeant Tillman knew that cold water pulls heat from a person's body. He worried about getting **hypothermia**. This condition is when a person's body temperature drops too low. As Tillman knew, a bad case of hypothermia can be deadly.

Danger Ahead

The jungle test began on the Yellow River in the Florida **Panhandle**. The men were divided into three groups. These were called Company A, Company B, and Company C. Tillman was part of Company B.

At noon on February 15, 1995, the trainees and their instructors climbed into rubber rafts. The three groups headed down the river. The water was only 52 **degrees**. If it had been just two degrees colder, the whole test would have been called off.

There was another danger, as well. Heavy rains had occurred in areas north of the Panhandle. The river was beginning to flood. No one in the group knew it, though. The floodwaters hadn't reached them yet. Again, if the instructors had known, they would have called off the test.

As the men floated down the river, they realized the water was rising. Company A's instructors sensed that it was too **risky** to continue ahead. They told their men to head for dry land. They would take a land route. Company B and Company C, however, headed farther down the river. They **plunged** into Crane Branch Swamp. They did not know that the waters of the swamp were dangerously high.

Ranger training involves many difficult tests.

The men realized as they floated that the water was rising.

Death in the Swamp

Tall, twisted trees rose more than 100 feet on all sides of the swamp. The air was heavy and moist. Soon, the two groups found dry land and left their rafts. But after walking many yards, they reached water again. Because they were still being tested, the trainees waded into the water.

The soldiers were surprised by how deep the water was. It was only supposed to be up to their ankles. Instead, the cold water came up to their waists. They banged their knees on tree stumps hidden in the water. They tripped over sunken roots. They stepped into deep holes. Thorn bushes cut them.

All that was bad enough. Then the cold water began to rise. It rose to their chests. Then it rose to their necks and beyond. The men put on life jackets to keep from drowning. They had to swim from tree to tree. As the sun set, some of the men began to shiver. It was a sign of hypothermia.

Until that point, the trainees had made their own decisions. But now the teachers were worried about the men's safety. So they took over. They told the

Sergeant Tillman gave his life saving his fellow soldiers.

soldiers to make a rope bridge over the deep water. One trainee would have to swim to the far side with the rope and tie it to a tree. Then one by one, the other trainees would move across the bridge.

Norman Tillman **volunteered** to be the last person in line. "You don't have to," said one of the instructors. "But I want to," answered Tillman.

So Sergeant Tillman stayed in the deep water, helping each man hook his safety line to the rope bridge. As he worked, he talked to himself. The men heard him saying, "Is it cold? Yeah, it's cold. Are you shivering? Oh, yeah, I'm shivering." Other men were shivering, too. Three of those men would soon die from hypothermia.

At last, only Tillman was left in the water. He untied the rope. Then the other soldiers pulled him across. They tried to get to dry land. By then, though, Tillman was suffering from **severe** hypothermia. His buddies tried to help him. But there was nothing they could do. By the time a helicopter arrived to rescue the soldiers, Norman Tillman was dead. His brave actions had helped save many lives.

USE WHAT YOU KNOW

Read and Remember — Finish the Sentence

Circle the best ending for each sentence.

1. The Yellow River was rising due to _____.
   a broken dam   melting ice   heavy rains

2. The group that took a land route was _____.
   Company A   Company B   Company C

3. The rising water made it hard for the men to see _____.
   hidden stumps   tall trees   their life jackets

4. Some trainees showed a sign of hypothermia when they _____.
   coughed   yawned   shivered

5. The men tried to cross a deep part of the swamp on a _____.
   float made from life jackets   rope bridge   log

6. Tillman helped soldiers hook on their _____.
   safety ropes   backpacks   boots

Think About It — Find the Sequence

Number the sentences to show the correct order from the story. The first one is done for you.

_____ **1.** Tillman's group entered Crane Branch Swamp.

_____ **2.** A helicopter arrived to rescue the soldiers.

__1__ **3.** The trainees were tested for mountain and desert fighting.

_____ **4.** The soldiers climbed into rubber rafts.

_____ **5.** Tillman offered to be the one to untie the rope.

_____ **6.** The remaining 102 trainees prepared for the jungle test.

Focus on Vocabulary — Make A Word

Choose a word in dark print to complete each sentence. Write the letters of the word on the blanks. When you are finished, the letters in the circles will tell what Sergeant Norman Tillman hoped to become.

volunteered	**instructors**	**severe**	**degrees**
plunged	**hypothermia**	**trainee**	**limit**
risky	**Panhandle**		

1. The jungle test was held in the Florida _____.

   ___ ___ ___ ___ ⭘ ___ ___ ___ ___

2. The cold water put Tillman in _____ danger.

   ___ ⭘ ___ ___ ___ ___

3. Each soldier was pushed to his _____.

   ___ ___ ⭘ ___ ___

4. It was _____, or dangerous, to enter the swamp.

   ___ ___ ___ ⭘ ___

5. The _____ became worried about the men's safety.

   ___ ___ ___ ___ ___ ___ ⭘ ___ ___ ___

6. Each remaining _____ would be tested for jungle fighting.

   ___ ___ ___ ___ ___ ⭘ ___ ___

7. Tillman _____, or offered, to be last in line.

   ___ ___ ___ ___ ___ ___ ___ ___ ⭘ ___

8. Companies B and C _____ into the swamp.

   ___ ___ ___ ___ ⭘ ___ ___

9. Being in cold water can cause a person to get _____.

   ___ ___ ___ ___ ___ ___ ___ ___ ⭘ ___ ___

10. The temperature of the river water was 52 _____.

    ___ ___ ⭘ ___ ___ ___ ___

Route Map

A **route map** shows the roads and highways in an area. The map key shows the symbols used for different kinds of roads and highways. The route map below is of the Florida Panhandle, where the Ranger training took place. Study the map and the map key. Write the answer to each question.

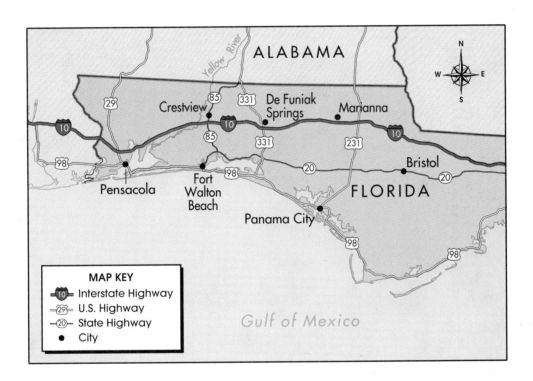

1. Which interstate highway runs east to west? _____

2. Which U.S. highway is along the coast? _____

3. Which state highway would you take to get from Crestview to Fort Walton Beach? _____

4. Which U.S. highway goes through De Funiak Springs? _____

5. What kind of highway goes through Bristol? _____

6. Which two highways meet in Pensacola? _____

Running for Their Lives

In 1993 **archaeologist** Peter Mathews made a great discovery. He was digging in the jungles of southern Mexico when he found a Mayan altar. The huge stone showed the ruler of a **civilization** from more than 1,200 years ago. Mathews quickly buried the altar again to keep it safe from robbers.

Four years later, Mathews returned to move the altar to a museum. But instead of getting the altar, Mathews ended up running for his life.

Whose Stone Is It?

After Mathews had found the altar, he told the Mexican government about it. He and the government leaders wanted to protect the altar. So they planned for Mathews to take the **ancient** stone to a museum in the town of Frontera Corozal.

Frontera Corozal was only about 25 miles away from El Cayo, the place where the altar was found. The Mayan **monument** would be safe in the museum and could be enjoyed by everyone. The plan was approved by Chol Indians in Frontera Corozal and in the nearby Mayan village of El Desempeño.

Mathews took ten men with him to rescue the altar. Three were Mexican archaeologists. The rest were Chol Indians from Frontera Corozal.

The group began digging up the monument on June 26, 1997. But the next morning, they were met by about sixty angry men from different villages. These villagers told Mathews to stop working. They said the El Cayo **ruins** and the monument belonged to them.

Ancient Mayan people sometimes made monuments to honor their rulers.

Mathews tried to tell them his plan. He tried to explain that he was only moving the altar to a museum. But it was no use. They wouldn't listen.

Big Trouble

A Chol Indian from El Desempeño tried to calm the villagers down. He had no luck. In fact, the angry villagers tied him to a tree. They did the same thing to one of Mathews's team when he spoke up.

At last, it became clear that the villagers were really **thieves**. They **demanded** all the money that Mathews's group had. They also took anything else they could sell. They even stole the boots off the feet of Mathews and his men. Then they told the frightened men to leave.

Mathews's group ran through the jungle to the shore of the Usumacinta River. As they ran, they heard shots ring out. A few of the thieves ordered them to stop and line up on the bank of the river. Mathews was afraid they would all be killed.

The thieves didn't shoot Mathews's team. But they did beat them up. Mathews and his men were badly injured. Then once again, the robbers told Mathews's group to leave. Otherwise, they said, they would kill all of them.

Escape Through the Jungle

None of the Chol Indians could swim. Six of them fled along the riverbank into the jungles to hide. The last one stayed with Mathews and the other archaeologists. This group decided to try to cross the river. That would take them across the **border** from Mexico to Guatemala. Perhaps there they would be safe. Luckily, they found an old canoe along the riverbank. They quietly crossed the river.

They were not out of danger yet, though. There was nothing but rain forest on this side of the river. Slowly, the men began walking through the dense trees and vines. They hoped to make it to a Guatemalan village called Piedras Negras. But it was hard to walk. Since

Mayan ruins can be found in many places in Mexico and Guatemala.

their boots had been stolen, their feet were bare. The men feared poisonous snakes. This jungle was full of them. Also, sharp thorns ripped their clothes and skin.

It began to rain. The men were cold and tired. But they were afraid to build a fire that night. They didn't want the thieves to see it and come after them again. They found water to drink but had no food.

The next morning, the men continued walking. They kept going all that day and most of the next. The **terrain** was very rough. In addition, the heavy rain caused the river to rise thirty feet. That made it almost impossible to walk along the riverbank.

At last, they were completely **exhausted**. They couldn't go any farther. "We were getting weaker and weaker," said Mathews. "It became clear we weren't going to make it to Piedras Negras."

The men sank down near the riverbank. They hoped a passing boat would see them. Luckily, a boat did come by and rescue them. At last, Peter Mathews and his friends were safe. But Mathews was in no rush to return to the jungle around the altar. He said, "I won't be going back to El Cayo for a while."

The men feared getting bit by a poisonous snake, such as this coral snake.

Read and Remember — Choose the Answer

Draw a circle around the correct answer.

1. Whose picture was on the altar that Mathews found?

an ancient Mayan ruler   a Chol Indian   a Spanish explorer

2. Why did Mathews bury the ancient altar again?

to protect it   to honor it   to destroy it

3. Where did Mathews want to take his discovery?

to Guatemala   to a government office   to Frontera Corozal

4. Who went to El Cayo to help Mathews?

government leaders   Chol Indians   Guatemalan villagers

5. What prevented Mathews's team from getting the monument?

Snakes covered it.   Heavy rains came.   Thieves came.

6. What did Mathews's group do after crossing the river?

built a fire   made a canoe   walked toward a village

Write About It

Imagine you were a newspaper reporter in 1997. Write a short article about Mathews's experience with the Mayan altar. Tell who, what, when, where, and why in your article.

_____

_____

_____

_____

_____

_____

USE WHAT YOU KNOW

Focus on Vocabulary — Crossword Puzzle

Use the clues to complete the puzzle. Choose from the words in dark print.

> **civilization**   **monument**   **ruins**   **terrain**
> **exhausted**   **archaeologist**   **ancient**   **thieves**
> **border**   **demanded**

Across

2. place where people work and share customs

5. person who studies past human life

8. remains of buildings from long ago

9. line that separates two countries

10. people who rob

Down

1. very tired

3. from long, long ago

4. asked for in a firm way

6. ground

7. statue made to honor a person

Distance Scale

On a map, use a **distance scale** to find the distance between two places. On this map of Mexico, the distance scale shows that 1 inch of the map stands for 300 miles of land. Use a ruler to measure the distances on the map. Circle the correct answer to each question.

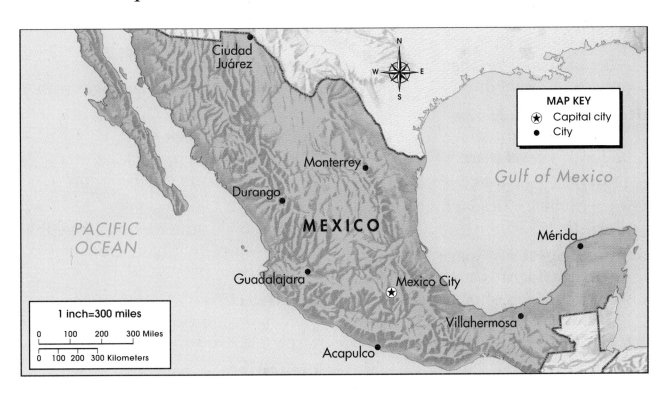

1. How many inches are between Mérida and Villahermosa on the map?

2 inches   3 inches   1 inch

2. What is the actual distance between Mérida and Villahermosa?

150 miles   225 miles   300 miles

3. What is the actual distance between Ciudad Juárez and Mexico City?

900 miles   625 miles   300 miles

4. Which city is about 375 miles from Guadalajara?

Acapulco   Monterrey   Durango

GLOSSARY

🌐 Words with this symbol can be found in the USE A MAP activities.

acres page 72
Acres are units for measuring land. An acre equals 43,560 square feet.

afford page 33
To afford means to be able to pay for, use, or be without.

allies page 64
Allies are countries that unite in order to do something.

altitude page 47
Altitude is height above sea level or another level place.

ancient page 95
Ancient means from a long time ago.

archaeologist page 95
An archaeologist is a scientist who studies the lives of people from long ago. He or she might study their bones, tools, or buildings.

avoided page 55
Avoided means stayed away from something or someone.

bamboo page 63
Bamboo is a tall grass that looks like tubes made of thin wood.

base page 47
A base is a place where an army keeps its supplies and where soldiers live.

blistered page 47
Blistered describes skin that has small bubbles filled with water.

border pages 53, 77, 97
🌐 A border is a line that separates two countries or other areas.

boundaries page 73
Boundaries are lines that mark the edges of an area of land or water.

braved page 42
Braved means faced danger with courage.

burden page 26
A burden is a heavy load that slows a person down.

canopy page 71
A canopy is the roof-like covering of treetops that have grown close together.

civilization page 95
A civilization is a place where people live and share customs.

clearing page 48
A clearing is a place where the land does not have any trees or brush.

climate page 57
Climate is the usual weather a place has.

coastal page 15
Coastal means near a seashore.

compass rose page 21
🌐 A compass rose is a symbol on a map that shows direction.

conditions   page 34
Conditions describes the way things are. Working conditions include pay, job hours, and work area.

contagious   page 33
Contagious means able to be passed easily from one person to another.

containers   page 33
Containers are objects, such as boxes or bottles, in which to put other things.

continent   pages 8, 13
🌎 A continent is a very large body of land, such as South America.

coop   page 32
A coop is a small building made to keep chickens or small animals.

coward   page 71
A coward is a person who is easily frightened.

crouching   page 17
Crouching means bending low.

current   page 24
A current is water moving in a certain direction.

customs   page 39
Customs are the ways people usually do things.

deforestation   page 72
Deforestation is the act of cutting down all the trees in an area of a forest.

degrees   pages 45, 85, 88
🌎 Degrees are units of measure for temperature or distance.

demanded   page 96
Demanded means asked for in a firm way.

dense   page 10
Dense means thick or packed close together.

desperation   page 9
Desperation is a feeling that comes when a person has lost all hope or needs something very badly.

diet   page 66
A diet is the usual food and drink that a person has.

dignity   page 57
To have dignity is to behave in a way that shows honor.

distance scale   pages 69, 101
🌎 A distance scale compares distance on a map with distance in the real world.

elevations   page 61
🌎 Elevations are heights above a given level, such as sea level.

equator   pages 29, 32
🌎 The equator is an imaginary circle that runs east and west around Earth. It divides Earth equally into north and south.

exhausted   page 98
Exhausted means very tired or worn out.

expedition   page 15
An expedition is a long journey taken for a reason, such as to explore an area.

extinct   page 55
Extinct means dead or gone. If an animal is extinct, all of its kind are gone.

fiber   page 65
Fiber is thread-like material from plants and trees.

fierce   page 17
Fierce means dangerous and strong.

foreigners   page 40
Foreigners are people who are from a different country.

former   page 23
Former means from the past.

grove   page 64
A grove is a small area full of trees but with few other plants.

habitat   page 55
A habitat is a place where an animal or a plant normally lives.

hack   page 81
To hack means to cut with heavy blows.

headwaters   page 23
Headwaters are small streams that form the beginning of a river.

heartbroken   page 58
Heartbroken means very sad.

hemispheres   page 29
If the world is divided in half, it is divided into two hemispheres.

hollow   page 16
A hollow is a place where the ground dips.

humid   page 32
Humid means damp.

hypothermia   page 87
Hypothermia is when a person's body temperature is very low. People in very cold air or water can be in danger of hypothermia.

infected   page 49
Infected means diseased.

injuries   page 47
Injuries are places on a person's body that are hurt or wounded.

instructors   page 87
Instructors are teachers.

latitude   pages 45, 85
Lines of latitude are imaginary lines that run east and west around Earth. They measure distance in degrees north and south of the equator.

ledge   page 81
A ledge is a rock that sticks out from the side of a mountain and looks like a narrow shelf.

legend   page 79
A legend is a story passed down over many years. It may or may not be true.

limit   page 87
A limit is a point that a person cannot go beyond.

livelier   page 40
Livelier means more full of life or more active.

local   page 39
Local means of a certain place.

longitude   pages 45, 85
Lines of longitude are imaginary lines that run north and south around Earth. They measure distance in degrees east and west of the 0° longitude.

map key   page 37
A map key tells what the symbols, colors, or patterns on a map mean.

mission   page 32
A mission is a place in another land where people teach their religion.

monument   page 95
A monument is a stone, building, or statue that is made to honor a person or an event.

mouth   page 39
A mouth is the place where a stream or river flows into a larger body of water, such as an ocean.

native   page 50
Native means originally from a certain place or country.

nephew   page 7
A nephew is the son of a person's brother or sister.

nomads   page 39
Nomads are people who do not live in one place but roam from one area to another.

officials   page 58
Officials are people in command.

panhandle   page 88
A panhandle is a narrow strip of land that sticks out from a larger area of land.

parachute   page 50
A parachute is a large piece of cloth that opens to catch wind and slow a person down.

patients   page 32
Patients are sick people who visit a doctor.

permission   page 7
Permission is the act of allowing a person to have or do something.

piranha   page 23
Piranha are small, dangerous fish with sharp teeth.

plains   page 39
Plains are large areas of flat land.

plunged   page 88
Plunged means pushed suddenly into water.

poisonous   page 23
Poisonous means causing sickness or death with poison.

portage   page 24
To portage means to carry boats or supplies over land.

porters   page 39
Porters are people who carry suitcases or equipment.

raft   page 9
A raft is a kind of flat boat that is sometimes made from pieces of wood.

rain forest   page 9
A rain forest is an area with many tall trees and a high amount of rain all year long. Most rain forests are near the equator.

range   page 55
A range is the area where an animal lives and travels.

rapids   page 24
Rapids are the fast-moving parts of a river.

ravine   page 79
A ravine is a narrow, deep valley between two walls of rock.

region   page 15
A region is an area of land.

remote   page 47
Remote means far away.

rescuer   page 81
A rescuer is a person who helps others who are hurt or are in dangerous places.

research   page 57
Research is information learned by studying a subject.

risky   page 88
Risky means possibly dangerous.

riverbanks   page 31
Riverbanks are the higher ground at the edges of rivers.

route map   page 93
A route map is a map that shows the roads and highways in an area.

ruins   page 95
Ruins are the remains of buildings and other objects that were destroyed a long time ago.

sap   page 71
Sap is the liquid in plants that carries food to the leaves and other parts.

search party   page 81
A search party is a group of people trying to find people who are lost.

severe   page 90
Severe means very serious.

slope   page 64
A slope is ground that slants.

smallpox   page 8
Smallpox is a dangerous disease. It can cause a high fever, a headache, a bad rash, and death.

soot   page 65
Soot is a fine black powder that is formed when something is burned.

S.O.S.   page 81
An S.O.S. is an emergency call or sign for help.

species   page 71
A species is a group of plants or animals that are all of the same kind.

spikes   page 18
Spikes are long, sharp pieces of wood or metal.

staggered   page 80
Staggered means walked in a shaky way.

stretchers   page 82
Stretchers are light beds that are used to carry people who are hurt.

summit   page 79
A summit is the highest point on a mountain.

surrender   page 64
To surrender means to give up.

survivors   page 48
Survivors are people who stay alive through a disaster, such as a flood or an airplane crash.

swamps   page 15
Swamps are lands that are wet, soft, and muddy. They are partly covered by water.

swarmed   page 41
Swarmed means flew or moved together in large numbers.

tailor   page 63
A tailor is a person who makes clothes.

tapper   page 71
A tapper is a person who makes small cuts in trees in order to collect sap or liquid from them.

terrain   page 98
Terrain is the surface of the land. It is hard to travel on rough terrain.

thieves   page 96
Thieves are people who rob.

threat   page 73
A threat is a dangerous person, animal, or object.

tornado   page 17
A tornado is a strong storm with high-speed, whirling winds. It is very dangerous and can destroy anything in its path.

trainee   page 87
A trainee is a person who is being trained or taught.

tributary   page 7
A tributary is a stream or river that flows into a larger stream or river.

tropical   page 63
Tropical describes a hot, wet area near the equator.

union   page 72
A union is a group of workers who join together to protect and improve their jobs.

unknown   page 15
Unknown means not known or not familiar.

urge   page 55
An urge is a strong wish to do something.

vampire bats   page 9
Vampire bats are bats that feed on blood from animals and sometimes people.

vegetation   page 24
Vegetation is plants.

volunteered   page 90
A person who volunteered to do something offered because he or she wanted to do it.

whirlpool   page 25
A whirlpool is fast-moving water that swirls in a circle.

Did You Know?

◀ Do you know where most of the world's tropical rain forests are? Over half are along the Amazon River in South America. One third are in Brazil alone!

How important are tropical rain ▶ forests? Scientists say that half of all plant and animal life on Earth lives in tropical rain forests. In fact, two square miles of rain forest may contain more than 40,000 different species of insects!

◀ How did the rain forest get its name? In tropical rain forests, it rains almost all year long! In fact, most tropical rain forests get about 100 inches of rain each year!

Did you know that rain forests are very dark? The dense, green canopy of treetops blocks out most of the sunlight. So very few plants grow on the ground of the rain forest! Thick tropical jungle plants need sun to grow. That means most of the rain forest is not true jungle! ▶

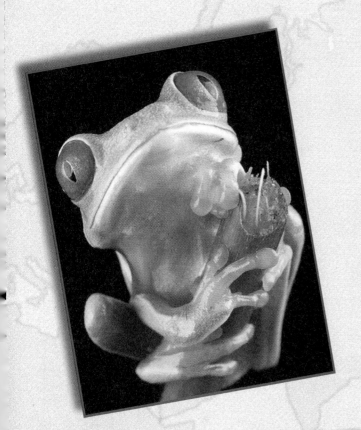

◀ Can you believe that some animals never touch the ground? Many kinds of tree frogs spend their whole lives in the trees of rain forests. As tadpoles, they swim in puddles on leaves. The adults stay in the trees eating insects!

◀ Have you ever wondered how strong leaves can be? The tropical Victoria regia water lily grows on the Amazon River. Its huge leaves are so strong that they can support a child's weight!

CHART YOUR SCORES

Score Your Work

1. Count the number of correct answers you have for each activity.
2. Write these numbers in the boxes in the chart.
3. Give yourself a score (maximum of 5 points) for **Write About It**.
4. Add up the numbers to get a final score for each tale.
5. Write your final score in the score box.
6. Compare your final score with the maximum score given for each story.

Tales	Read and Remember	Think About It	Write About It	Focus on Vocabulary	Use a Map	Score
Lost in the Rain Forest						/25
African Adventurer						/22
River of Doubt						/23
Jungle Doctor						/24
Across Africa						/26
Plane Crash in the Jungle						/27
Saving the Mountain Gorillas						/22
28 Years in the Jungle						/25
Rain Forest Hero						/24
The Place of the Dead						/22
Pushed to the Limit						/28
Running for Their Lives						/25

ANSWER KEY

Lost in the Rain Forest

Pages 6–13
Read and Remember — Finish the Sentence:
1. riding in a canoe 2. ran away 3. steer a canoe
4. Indians 5. France
Think About It — Drawing Conclusions:
1. Her husband was there. 2. Smallpox had killed
everyone in the town. 3. Answers should include
two of the following: They ran out of food. They
were sick from disease. Vampire bats attacked them.
There was no fresh water to drink. 4. After four
weeks, they realized that help might never come.
Focus on Vocabulary — Finish the Paragraphs:
1. continent 2. permission 3. nephew 4. tributary
5. smallpox 6. vampire bats 7. raft 8. desperation
9. rain forest 10. dense
Use a Map — Continents and Oceans:
1. South America, North America, Africa, Asia,
Europe, Australia, Antarctica 2. North America,
South America, Antarctica 3. Atlantic Ocean, Arctic
Ocean 4. Indian Ocean, Pacific Ocean 5. Africa,
Asia, Australia, Antarctica 6. Atlantic Ocean

African Adventurer

Pages 14–21
Read and Remember — Check the Events:
Sentences 1, 4, 6
Write About It: Answers will vary.
Focus on Vocabulary — Match Up:
1. d 2. i 3. h 4. g 5. b 6. e 7. a 8. j 9. c 10. f
Use a Map — Map Directions:
1. north 2. east 3. southeast 4. northeast

River of Doubt

Pages 22–29
Read and Remember — Choose the Answer:
1. Candido Rondon 2. to map the river
3. rapids 4. in a whirlpool 5. He became sick.
6. Rio Roosevelt
Think About It — Find the Main Ideas:
Sentences 1, 5
Focus on Vocabulary — Crossword Puzzle:
ACROSS — 4. portage 6. current 8. headwaters
9. piranha 10. poisonous; DOWN — 1. burden
2. vegetation 3. former 5. whirlpool 7. rapids

Use a Map — Hemispheres:
1. Southern Hemisphere 2. Eastern Hemisphere
3. equator 4. Western Hemisphere, Northern
Hemisphere, and Southern Hemisphere 5. Eastern
Hemisphere, Southern Hemisphere

Jungle Doctor

Pages 30–37
Read and Remember — Check the Events:
Sentences 3, 4, 6
Write About It: Answers will vary.
Focus on Vocabulary — Finish Up:
1. riverbanks 2. mission 3. equator 4. contagious
5. coop 6. patients 7. humid 8. conditions
9. containers 10. afford
Use a Map — Map Keys:
1. ▲ 2. no 3. large city 4. Ogooué River
5. Lambaréné, Oyem, Mouila 6. two

Across Africa

Pages 38–45
Read and Remember — Finish the Sentence:
1. Kenya 2. a donkey 3. food she had bought
4. rest houses 5. by joining them 6. west
Think About It — Fact or Opinion:
1. F 2. F 3. O 4. O 5. F 6. O
Focus on Vocabulary — Make a Word:
1. swarmed 2. braved 3. customs 4. mouth
5. nomads 6. foreigners 7. porters 8. livelier
9. local 10. plains
The letters in the circles spell *West Africa*.
Use a Map — Latitude and Longitude:
1. 41°N 2. 99°W 3. Port Moresby 4. Mount Kenya

Plane Crash in the Jungle

Pages 46–53
Read and Remember — Choose the Answer:
1. near Hidden Valley 2. twenty-one 3. with a
mirror 4. He dipped the wings. 5. dense trees
6. food
Write About It: Answers will vary.
Focus on Vocabulary — Find the Meaning:
1. far away 2. Army station 3. height above the
ground 4. covered with small bubbles 5. wounds
6. people who lived 7. open area 8. diseased

9. cloth used to slow a person in air 10. originally living there

Use a Map — Countries:
1. Port Moresby 2. Darwin, Brisbane 3. Indonesia
4. Indonesia 5. Malaysia 6. Papua New Guinea

Saving the Mountain Gorillas

Pages 54–61

Read and Remember — Check the Events:
Sentences 2, 4, 6

Think About It — Cause and Effect:
1. c 2. a 3. e 4. b 5. d

Focus on Vocabulary — Finish the Paragraphs:
1. urge 2. extinct 3. habitat 4. range 5. climate
6. avoided 7. dignity 8. heartbroken 9. officials
10. research

Use a Map — Elevation:
1. dark green 2. 0–1,650 feet 3. Dar es Salaam
4. above 18,000 feet

28 Years in the Jungle

Pages 62–69

Read and Remember — Finish the Sentence:
1. Japan 2. an underground cave 3. tree bark
4. continued to hide 5. fishermen 6. a hero's welcome

Write About It: Answers will vary.

Focus on Vocabulary — Match Up:
1. f 2. g 3. c 4. h 5. e 6. b 7. j 8. a 9. d 10. i

Use a Map — Distance Scale:
1. 1 inch 2. 10 miles 3. 26 miles 4. New Agat

Rain Forest Hero

Pages 70–77

Read and Remember — Choose the Answer:
1. Brazil 2. open spaces 3. the burning season
4. ranchers 5. peacefully 6. He was shot to death.

Think About It — Find the Main Ideas:
Sentences 2, 5

Focus on Vocabulary — Find the Meaning:
1. frightened person 2. kinds 3. covering of treetops 4. person who draws liquid 5. liquid food
6. units of measure for land 7. group of workers
8. clearing away of trees 9. limits 10. danger

Use a Map — Countries:
1. Bogotá 2. French Guiana, Brazil, Guyana
3. Brazil 4. French Guiana 5. Xapuri 6. yes

The Place of the Dead

Pages 78–85

Read and Remember — Check the Events:
Sentences 1, 4, 6

Write About It: Answers will vary.

Focus on Vocabulary — Finish Up:
1. S.O.S. 2. staggered 3. legend 4. hack 5. rescuer
6. summit 7. ledge 8. search party 9. ravine
10. stretchers

Use a Map — Latitude and Longitude:
1. Banjarmasin 2. Pontianak 3. 122°E
4. Ujungpandang

Pushed to the Limit

Pages 86–93

Read and Remember — Finish the Sentence:
1. heavy rains 2. Company A 3. hidden stumps
4. shivered 5. rope bridge 6. safety ropes

Think About It — Find the Sequence: 4, 6, 1, 3, 5, 2

Focus on Vocabulary — Make a Word:
1. Panhandle 2. severe 3. limit 4. risky
5. instructors 6. trainee 7. volunteered
8. plunged 9. hypothermia 10. degrees
The letters in the circles spell *Army Ranger*.

Use a Map — Route Map:
1. Interstate Highway 10 2. U.S. Highway 98
3. State Highway 85 4. U.S. Highway 331
5. state highway 6. U.S. Highways 29 and 98

Running for Their Lives

Pages 94–101

Read and Remember — Choose the Answer:
1. an ancient Mayan ruler 2. to protect it
3. to Frontera Corozal 4. Chol Indians
5. Thieves came. 6. walked toward a village

Write About It: Answers will vary.

Focus on Vocabulary — Crossword Puzzle:
ACROSS — 2. civilization 5. archaeologist 8. ruins
9. border 10. thieves; DOWN — 1. exhausted
3. ancient 4. demanded 6. terrain 7. monument

Use a Map — Distance Scale:
1. 1 inch 2. 300 miles 3. 900 miles 4. Monterrey